"You'll start giggling and end up pondering deep biblical truth."
—Lynn D. Morrissey, popular speaker and author of *Love Letters to God*

"The most unique and refreshing devotional for women I've read in years!"
—Ellie Kay, bestselling author of *A Woman's Guide to Family Finances*

"Rachel's writing matches who she really is—empathetic, insightful, unconventional, and very funny."
—Lindsey O'Connor, bestselling author of *If Mama Ain't Happy, Ain't Nobody Happy*

"Rachel is a gifted communicator, sharing God's truth with unconventional wit."
—Jane Jarrell, author of *Secrets of a Midlife Mom* and *The Frazzle Factor*

"Certifiably hilarious, vulnerable, and encouraging. Rachel is the new Christian humor writer to watch!"
—Becky Freeman, award-winning humorist and bestselling author of *Help! I'm Turning into My Mother!*

WAKE
UP
Laughing

WAKE UP Laughing

OFFBEAT DEVOTIONS FOR THE "UNCONVENTIONAL" WOMAN

Rachel St. John-Gilbert

BARBOUR
PUBLISHING

Published in association with the literary agency of Alive Communications, Inc., 7680 Goddard Street, Suite 200, Colorado Springs, Colorado 80920.

Published by Barbour Publishing, Inc., P.O. Box 719, Uhrichsville, Ohio 44683, www.barbourbooks.com

Our mission is to publish and distribute inspirational products offering exceptional value and biblical encouragement to the masses.

 Member of the
Evangelical Christian
Publishers Association

Printed in China.

DEDICATION

To my precious family:
Scott, Trevor Scott, Tori Leigh,
and Whitney Nicole.
We may not always wake up laughing,
but we sure come close.

ACKNOWLEDGMENTS

This book would be a few disjointed essays gathering dust in a shoe box in the top of my closet if it weren't for a moment of kismet over dinner with several writing friends. During dinner, at one point I lifted my fork and pointed it squarely at editor-guru Steve Laube and asked, "Why can't Christian women wake up laughing?"

Before the last word left my lips, he and fellow diner, author Becky Freeman, locked eyes and sang in unison, "That's your title!"

Later, both friends came through at critical junctures and not only kept the project alive but kept my hopes alive that this book would make it to publication—eventually. A year later and days after I delivered my "If Your idea of expanding my territory is letting my Pulitzer Prize contender hang out in the top of my closet, that is A-okay with me" speech to God, Shannon Hill with Barbour Publishing rode in on a white horse with contract in hand.

Warm appreciation to Super Agent Man, Lee Hough. James Bond has nothing on you. Your wisdom and friendship have steadied me throughout this sometimes-daunting process. It still amazes me that you answer my phone calls. (Okay, so I use the pseudonym of "Stormie Omartian," but still. . .)

Thanks, too, to our babysitting crew who rode herd on our herd: Kristi and Jenny Pereira and wonder dog, Penny; Lauren Schleyer; and Britney Spears (I mean, Meyer). Our kids have been blessed by your enthusiasm, kindness, and creativity.

And finally, heartfelt gratitude to the hired hands and big hearts of my substantive editors: lead editor (and sometimes collaborator), my mother and bestselling author, Ruthie Arnold; and coeditor/author, Lynn D. Morrissey (check out her exquisitely written book on prayer journaling: *Love Letters to God*). Both women kept me in stitches with their funnies, in tears with their genuine encouragement, and in awe of their giftedness.

Even so, my greatest awe is reserved for God. His love sets me free, draws me into Him, and keeps me laughing.

CONTENTS

FOREWORD

Every morning as we slip out of bed and slide our feet into our warm fluffy slippers, we have a choice. Will we face the circumstances and people in our life with grumbling and negativity—or will we face them with gratitude? The choice is ours! The attitude we choose will color our day.

I grant you that it's easier to let life's challenges get the better of us, causing us to whine and complain in despair. It's more difficult to choose to rejoice when situations and people don't exactly fit into our personal picture of how life should be.

Each of us could use a little help and encouragement in seeing the positive side of life. That's what Rachel St. John-Gilbert has given us. *Wake Up Laughing* is more than a devotional book—it's a jump start to our day! Through her candid examples we learn to laugh at situations that might normally make us worry, fret, or cry. We learn to take off the dark glasses of despair and put on the bright glasses of hope to see every circumstance as an opportunity to learn and draw closer to God.

As you read this creative and unique book of devotions, you'll begin to experience your world in a fresh new way. You'll be encouraged to allow the glorious light of laughter to lighten the path of some of your darker situations. You'll discover yourself in the "unconventional" reality of Rachel's world—personally I take great comfort in the fact that I'm not the only one who gets nervous ordering coffee at Starbucks!

Some of life's greatest lessons are learned through laughter, so take a walk on the lighter side of life and enjoy a daily dose of devotional delight!

KAROL LADD
Author of the best-selling books
The Power of a Positive Wife,
The Power of a Positive Mom,
and *The Power of a Positive Friend*

Introduction

THE PURPOSE-DRIVEN LAUGH

While shopping at a Christian bookstore, I overheard a genteel Southern lady asking a friend, "Have you read that *wundaful* new book called *The Purpose-Driven Laugh?*"

I thought, *Wow, what a great title. I need to get a copy.* Well, as it turns out, she was actually looking for Rick Warren's *The Purpose-Driven Life.* But I started thinking, *Does laughter have a meaningful purpose in our lives, or is it just a frivolous physical phenomenon that matters little when the giggles have faded into silence?* And then I thought some more.

Life gives us many opportunities to be solemn and contemplative—whether we're facing guilt from blowing our tops at cranky toddlers, mouthy teens, or aggravating spouses; wringing our hands over today's troubling headlines; or reeling from the loss of someone we love. But if we succumb to the heaviness we feel, the enemy often places one foot squarely on our hearts and the other on our funny bones—and we end up immobilized.

However, if we can wrestle free to embrace the

concept that something about God's gift of laughter is primal and life infusing, we have a fighting chance to rise above the troubles that threaten to steal our joy. Proverbs 17:22 promises, "A cheerful heart is good medicine." In fact, studies have shown that laughter releases endorphins from our brains to boost our bodies' healing process. Frequent laughter helps control pain, lower blood pressure, and relieve stress. Perhaps our bodies don't need a healing edge, but many of our spirits do.

Many years ago, an obscure monk, Brother Lawrence, implored his fellow Christians to "practice the presence" of God in the routine tasks of their lives. He had found that this practice helps us see God more often and more clearly. I'm no Brother Lawrence, but I do sense God's presence in the ordinary experiences of daily life, often through His divine sense of humor.

These devotional essays may be offbeat, but they also reflect the belief that God has a sense of humor. Indeed, it was God who told Sarah to name her baby "Isaac," whose literal meaning is "laughter." As Terry Lindvall points out in his book *The Mother of All Laughter: Sarah and the Genesis of Comedy*, philosopher Ted Cohen asks why God directed Abraham to sacrifice a ram and free Isaac: "Is not God Himself directing that laughter be freed and let loose in the world?"

Additionally, did you know that children laugh about four hundred times a day and adults only about fifteen? The scriptures teach that unless we become as little children, we cannot see the kingdom of God. I can't help but wonder if the downward spiral of our daily laugh quotient as we "mature" is a hindrance to our ability to experience God's presence.

I'm convinced God has woven His distinct sense of humor into the fabric of our daily lives so that we may experience His presence in a personal way. It is my joy and privilege to hold up a magnifying glass so we can revel in the comedic and quirky details together.

As you read these devotional thoughts—whether morning, noon, or night—I hope your spirit will be uplifted through a smile, chuckle, or belly laugh. And more than that, I hope you will look forward to your quiet time each day with the Creator of laughter (well, it *used* to be quiet). May your heart overflow with gratitude as He fills up your endorphin tank, equipping you to face the serious side of life with grace and courage.

Chapter 1

RICH BARBIE, POOR BARBIE
The Comparison Trap

As a child, did you ever have a nemesis—someone you liked but who always seemed to be "one up" on you? If you ran a block, she ran two; if you got a trike, she got a bike. And if you made an A, she made an A+.

Each fall, *my* neighborhood nemesis, Tammy, and I eagerly waited for the Sears catalog to arrive. When it finally did, we circled our Christmas wish lists with an ink pen, beginning with the toy page, then moving on to bikes and eventually to home furnishings (you're never too young to register your china pattern, you know).

One year when I was about six years old, I asked for the Super Barbie Camping Van, partly because it fit my tomboy personality. But make no mistake, tomboy or no, I (vicariously through my Barbie doll) still had my cap set on Ken. I felt that he, being an outdoorsy sort of guy, would really dig my new camper.

So that Christmas morning, I proudly hauled my brand-spanking-new orange and pink Super Barbie Camper down the street to Tammy's house. I knew she had asked for a Barbie house, but I was reasonably sure it was too expensive, even for Tammy's family. And besides, I was happy with my tranformable van with pull-out couch, beds, and funky fuzzy accent pillows. Yes, I was satisfied until. . .I walked into Tammy's bedroom. There before my widened eyes was the mama of all Barbie houses—a three-storied Super Barbie Penthouse with working elevator. Suddenly, my warm contentment was chilled like the champagne in Rich Barbie's ice bucket. I tried to take it all in stride. After all, my Barbie now had the richest friend in Barbie World. She would not only get to ride in Rich Barbie's penthouse elevator but also ride shotgun in Rich Barbie's silver convertible.

However, as Tammy and I played together that Christmas Day, I couldn't shake the feeling of being one-upped again. While Tammy's Barbie mixed cocktails and grilled salmon for a seaside date with Ken, *my* Barbie mixed lemonade and grilled cheese sandwiches on her camper stove at the local KOA campground. To take the one-upmanship a notch higher, Tammy had enough outfits and accessories to fill a dozen shoe boxes. On any given day, Rich Barbie could offer Ken a trip to the

Alps for skiing, a jaunt to Cancun for sunning, or a visit to the English countryside for horseback riding. And she could provide equipment and matching outfits for both of them. While Rich Barbie was whisking Ken to the airport in her convertible, Poor Barbie was back at camp, cleaning the van's port-a-potty.

In about an hour, the joy of my new toy had dissipated into discontent. It wasn't that I wanted the penthouse but more that Tammy had a way of flaunting her stuff and insinuating that *her* Barbie and trappings were better than mine. And worse yet, that her stuff would make a happier Ken.

I'm now almost forty years old. I have to confess that sometimes I'm not too far removed from the six-year-old girl I used to be, who often felt like Secondhand Rose in Tammy's presence. Why is it so easy to feel small and insecure around others who have bigger, better houses, cars, clothes, and grown-up toys?

The Bible clearly says where our treasure is, there our hearts will be also (Matthew 6:21). That sounds good in sermons but is hard to embrace in real life. The Bible also says our lives are only vapors (James 4:14), but we don't see it that way. It's hard to train our hearts and spirits to look past this world and all it offers our senses and to envision a reality we can't see. But God calls us to a higher standard that will set our spirits free.

Sometimes it helps to remind ourselves that we probably have friends who have less than *we* have and fight their own battles of feeling inferior about *us*. May our Father teach us simply to love the people He places us with and to watch for and perhaps help with *their* needs and pain, for richer or poorer.

Love is patient, love is kind. It does not envy, it does not boast, it is not proud. . . . It always protects, always trusts, always hopes, always perseveres. Love never fails.
1 Corinthians 13:4, 7–8

Chapter 2

THE MIDDLE AGES
Coming of Middle Age

Tonight as I stood in the grocery store checkout line, I had a Coming of Middle Age experience. I surveyed the contents of my cart, and the realization hit me like a ton of Metamucil: I was about to purchase my first pillbox. No wimpy seven-compartment pillbox for *me*. No, sirree. Nothing but the most advanced state-of-the-art deluxe pillbox for *this* tough old bird. Yes, my little plastic health helper is a real beauty in aqua green with four compartments per day for a total of twenty-eight tidy squares to hold the answers to all that ails me.

I could hardly believe my eyes. I had just eked out my last child, only to run headlong into the maintenance-heavy middle ages. Only yesterday I was holding my newborn baby! How could I, only a year later, possibly be old enough to take enough supplements and medication to require such a square possession?

It's not like I'm on enough drugs to warrant a field trip to the Betty Ford Clinic. Most of my pills are vitamin supplements to keep my cholesterol numbers in check. Still, it seems that just as I get one pesky condition under control, another pops up. It's like that arcade game where you whack a mole back into his hole, but it's impossible to keep him down. He keeps coming back like last year's fruitcake.

And another thing: Why do they call it *middle age* anyway? *My* theory is that we reach the age where our middle becomes the focus of our lives—bulging and expanding like an inflatable swimming ring with a mind of its own. Other signs of approaching middle age include transitioning from 100 percent cotton undies to 100 percent spandex; rolling out the welcome mat for our "irregular" monthly visitor, now cycling through about twice as often as we're used to; and having enough spider veins in our legs to resemble a walking atlas.

If you're a midlife mommy, things get even more interesting. I have to tell you that my heart leaps when I see a woman with a few gray hairs and crow's-feet, holding a baby who is clearly hers—and not her grandchild. It's nice to know I won't be the only mother attending PTA who will probably be mistaken for my child's grandmother and that my husband and I will not be the only parents hovering near sixty when our last child graduates from high school. So much for those idyllic empty-nest years!

Whether or not you are staring down the maw of middle age, you may be facing other life or bodily changes that remind you that things don't stay the same for very long. Change can be unsettling or it can be revitalizing, but we'd do best to make our peace with constant change. The only thing we can absolutely count on in life is change. As I realize I'm getting older and my body is showing it, the idea of my mortality is more real and not so far off.

My mom says that as she gets further down the road, Jesus has proved to be all He promises to be. I find that reassuring. As missionary Jim Elliot has taught us, why wouldn't we give up things that we cannot keep for all that—in Christ—we cannot lose?

Swift to its close ebbs out life's little day;
Earth's joys grow dim, its glories pass away;
Change and decay in all around I see.
O Thou who changest not, abide with me.
"ABIDE WITH ME," HENRY LYTE, 1820

So will it be with the resurrection of the dead. The body that
is sown is perishable, it is raised imperishable; it is sown in
dishonor, it is raised in glory; it is sown in weakness, it is raised
in power; it is sown a natural body, it is raised a spiritual body.
1 CORINTHIANS 15:42–44

Chapter 3

NOT-SO-TECHNICAL DIFFICULTIES
When Life Gives You Lemons

Recently I was reading *AARP* magazine. Not because I'm over fifty, but because I love to say AARP over and over again and pretend I'm a seal. Try it. Say it three times fast, and trust me, you'll be clapping your hands and demanding fish for dinner in no time.

A bit of frustrated actress is left in me from my portrayal of poker-playing Mrs. O'Malley in the Shackelford Junior High production of *Funny Girl*. Being a star, I enjoy reading about my peers. So, as I was reading the *AARP* magazine, an interview with British actor Michael Caine caught my attention. Although our ideologies don't move in parallel lines, I admire the fact that he's been married to the same woman for twenty-seven years (a rarity in our business) and that, vocationally, he has reached for the stars—indeed, become a star—despite growing up in poverty.

In the interview, the sixty-seven-year-old Caine was asked, "Do you have fatherly advice for your daughters?" He answered, "I was in rehearsals, waiting behind a door to come out while a couple onstage were having a row. They starting throwing furniture, and a chair lodged in front of the door. My cue came, and I could only get halfway in. I stopped and said, 'I can't get in. The chair's in the way.' And the producer said, 'Use the difficulty.' I said, 'What do you mean?' And he said, 'Well, if it's a drama, pick it up and smash it. If it's a comedy, fall over it.'"

Don't you love it? I'm pragmatic, and at times my pragmatism used to slide into negativism. Well, God graciously saw fit to put some optimistic "producers" and "directors" in my life who have penetrated my pragmatism with sunshiny rays of encouragement in the face of cold, hard obstacles. And the mind-set of looking for redeeming qualities amid difficult circumstances brought a big paradigm shift for me.

If this sounds intriguing, and if you didn't participate in the seal barking exercise above, here's another chance to join in. Think of an obstacle you are facing, and put a positive face on it. Lost your job? Thank God for a season to spend extra precious time with your children. Moving? Revel in the fact that you have an instant new wardrobe (no one in your new town has seen your old duds).

See what I mean?

What do you think? It might be kind of fun to discover a positive for every negative event that life can throw at you. "Use the difficulty" to your advantage and to God's glory. So go ahead—take whatever is blocking your ability to move forward onto the Stage of Life with confidence and poise, and use it!

And we know that in all things God works for the good of those who love him, who have been called according to his purpose.
ROMANS 8:28

Chapter 4

CREEPY CRAWLER
An Appetite Only God Can Satisfy

When our baby Whitney started crawling, I was thrilled that she was right on target with her developmental skills. Our whole family passed more than a few happy hours (the merry kind—not the bar kind) observing the evolution of her movement.

We dubbed Phase One the precrawling David Copperfield Stage: I would set her by a pile of pillows on the floor and moments later find her several feet away from her original spot—and I didn't have a clue how she had transported herself to her new locale. Phase Two was the Dog-at-Fire-Hydrant Stage: Whitney would get in the traditional four-on-the-floor stance, then push up on one hind leg. This position was not the height of femininity, but it was entertaining and thankfully the phase was short-lived. By Phase Three, she had moved on to Cookin' with Crisco, as we say in Texas. She motored about the family room as if powered by petrol rather than strained peas and carrots.

Once I realized that Whitney could no longer be confined to her pile of toys on the den carpet, I had a face-to-face with her. "Now, sweetie, with every privilege comes responsibility. So I know you won't disappoint your father and me by using your crawling skills to find things to put in your mouth that don't belong there—right?"

Chubby-cheeked, bright-eyed Whitney beamed at me with her mouth open and a droplet of drool running down her chin. I took this as a "Yes, ma'am."

So I set Miss Whitney in a sea of toys in her usual place on the den carpet. Later I looked to make sure she wasn't gumming nonapproved items. At first glance, all appeared well. Baby was sitting happily Indian-style amid the toys and amusing herself by thrusting her little legs outward one at a time, symbolizing sheer delight. But the closer I got, the more uneasy I became. *What is that black string hanging out of her mouth?* I wondered for a split second before dashing into my "I'm going in after it" stance.

As I crouched on my hands and knees, her face came into focus, and her jaw shut like a steel trap. She turned from me to protect her treasure. Growing increasingly uneasy, I turned her face toward mine and saw the serrated edges of a cricket's hind leg dangling from the side of my daughter's mouth. More recently, I found Whitney casually sucking on the behind of the most beautiful metallic blue beetle as if it were a Tic Tac. The head was a goner, but he must have been gorgeous, judging from the other end.

Why is it that we mothers (grandmothers, aunts, and babysitters) can set a baby amid a hundred primary-colored, squeaking toys—totaling about a thousand dollars in the best that Toys"R"Us offers—only to find the little toot scarfing down common household pests the moment we turn our backs?

I've decided I'll make a million with my own line of bug-flavored baby food. How about "Peas, Carrots, and Roly-Polys"? Or "Summer Squash with Silverfish"? Maybe if we give babies what they really want, they'll stop hankering for what's off-limits. It just might work.

We surround ourselves with the run-of-the-mill accoutrements of life, but in the end, we can't squelch that primal longing for something more—something "outside the toy box" that calls to us. Do you struggle with feelings of discontent? Do you wonder if life offers more than what you're experiencing? Listen to that primal urge deep within. It's there by design and can only be filled with God.

"I am the way and the truth and the life.
No one comes to the Father except through me."

JOHN 14:6

GO FISH
Baiting the Hook for Life's Best

I unashamedly admit that I have often envied a local journalist who writes restaurant and entertainment reviews for our paper—one who looks every bit like a glamorous writer should: Short blond hair frames a classically pretty face, radiating a Joan Lunden smile. "Ahh," the dreamer in me sighs, "perhaps one day I could look like that." Then the realist in me retorts, "Yeah, right. Maybe after a gallon of bleach and a round of Botox."

I was particularly taken with "Joan's" review of a Vietnamese noodle house that had just opened in our town. "Hey!" The pragmatist me took over. "If I can't look like this lady, I can certainly eat like she does." I grabbed my keys and took off.

Once I was snuggled comfortably in my seat, the waiter appeared, and I whipped out the review. Pointing to Joan's picture, I said, "I'll have what she had."

There I was at Pho Garden Noodle House, having what that attractive together-looking writer had and feeling very journalistic. My waiter softly and swiftly served my chicken noodle soup piping hot in a large ceramic bowl along with a ten-inch replica of a fishing boat. It was filled with bean sprouts, cilantro, and bay leaves. Hmm. Not quite sure what to do with the leafy boat, I decided to wait a few moments and see if my timid waiter might also bring a miniature fishing pole and bucket of minnows.

Several minutes passed, and not one but two dark-haired, friendly waiters saw my quandary and decided to brief me on Vietnamese boating etiquette. Bowing and beaming, they advised me to pull the leaves off the basil, then season to taste with the desired amount of sprouts and cilantro. I thanked them but couldn't resist suggesting they consider the minnow bucket idea or at the very least a tiny container of stink bait.

"After all," I said seriously, "this *is* a Texas fishing town."

The Smiley Brothers backed toward the kitchen in unison, their smiles now appearing uneasy. They kept their eyes on me and whispered to each other from the corners of their mouths as they went. All in all, it was a fun afternoon disturbing the peace at Pho Garden. And seriously, my local Joan Lunden actually inspired me to expand my culinary and cultural horizons. Although I am squarely and happily stuck in Mommy Land most of the time, I enjoyed tracing the footsteps of a local semicelebrity and dining like the "other half," if only for an afternoon.

When we see a person we envy or imagine as living the perfect life, it may signal that there are latent gifts within us that we aren't using. Maybe there are experiences we should pursue that will enrich our lives and bring glory to God. Spiritual maturity is partly about turning the yearning into positive action. With God's perspective, we can move from envy to inspiration— from Stuck-in-a-Rut Woman to Can-Do Gal. Perhaps there is someone *you* admire from afar who will propel you toward new experiences, new ministry, or even a new career.

God has a plan for all of us, unique to our gifts and temperaments. Part of the secret of a fulfilling life is tapping into His template for us. If you feel a twinge of longing when you look at someone's accomplishments, think about my miniature fishing boat. Grab the spiritual "fishing pole" of action, tempered with prayer, and go fish for the life that God has specifically designed for you.

On the other hand, if you're a rare individual who feels you're exactly where God has placed you, then at *least* find a nice, dignified restaurant some afternoon and see if you can shake up the waiters a little.

Do not neglect your gift....
Be diligent in these matters;
give yourself wholly to them.
1 TIMOTHY 4:14–15

Chapter 6

CLASSY MOMS
Making Peace with Your Social Niche

Before my last baby girl was born, I was drawn to the cover of Martha Stewart's *Baby* magazine. I'm a patsy for photos of adorable babies dressed in cotton fabrics in shades of robin-egg blue, soft mint green, and melon. Yet if I'm completely honest, underneath my appreciation for the adorable pictures of pastel-clad babies lies a twinge of envy.

The picture-perfect life of well-dressed wee ones chowing down on organic baby food and hanging out in designer-decorated nurseries hit me with a sense of longing. The fact that the babies were invariably being cuddled by flat-tummied mommies who dined on soy shakes and celery appealed to me, too, in spite of being completely outside the realm of reality for moi et mini-moi. I mean, who among us as young, single gals didn't fantasize about marrying a JFK Jr. look-alike with enough dough to land us in a quaint Nantucket cottage, filling our days canning fruits and vegetables from a white-picket-fence garden?

Then real life happens. If we're lucky, hubby resembles a distant, homely cousin of John John. And chances are that our homes are closer to Walmart than the Atlantic, and our days are filled separating Play-Doh crumbs from carpet fibers rather than clipping herbs from the garden. And thus we realize early on that money makes a difference, and we never seem to have enough. So we find mommies of like ilk and while away the toddler years at trendy haunts like McDonald's Playland.

Just when I had accepted the fact that I was contentedly nestling into my spot on the lower-middle rung of America's class system, an article challenged my view. I read an interview with a well-heeled novelist who was still raising youngish children, and I realized she and I might have some things in common:

Q: Any plans for summer vacation? I hear you're an avid birder.

A: I try to include my kids in all kinds of mundane things and make them interesting.

(So far, so good, I thought, bonding with my newfound upper-class literary counterpart.) For my son, I felt I needed some hobbies to do with him. So when I saw that he had a little interest in birds, I turned the whole family into birders. *(How sweet, my kids love birds, too! She's my kind of gal. See? Nothing separates the elite from the commoners, after all.)* We've been taking adventure trips the last five or six years to Peru, Chile, and Galapagos. *(Uh-oh. Good-bye, my newfound friend. The only Chile my kids will ever see is in a bowl with beans,* I realized as I closed the magazine.)

Okay, so maybe economics does separate people. And to be perfectly honest, even if I could afford a weekly body wrap and mud bath, I don't think it would be my cup of tea; I would feel like a human burrito headed to soak in refried beans.

Our family videos may never conjure images of the square-jawed Kennedy clan in V-neck sweaters tossing a football on a wind-swept beach. But I'm grateful for my little place in the sun with a loving husband, healthy children, and a middle-class lifestyle that most of the free world envies.

The next time you're tempted to covet the good life, think again. Compared to many people, you're probably already living it. Why not try hard to be thankful for all God has given you? Decide to make an impact for Him in the unique circle of influence where He has placed you and your sweet family.

Okay then. Wanna meet me at McDonald's?

Keep your lives free from the love of money and be content with what you have, because God has said, "Never will I leave you; never will I forsake you."
Hebrews 13:5

Chapter 7

A WEIGHTY SUBJECT
Can't Get No Satisfaction?

Oh, the things we'll do to save a calorie! Not long ago, we thought rice cakes would answer all of our snacking dilemmas. Even though they tasted like butter-flavored Styrofoam, we scarfed down the dry, bumpy disks with abandon, certain they would keep us out of the potato chip bag and on the straight and narrow with the scales. But if you're like me, you reached for the chips anyway after eating an entire bag of rice cakes. So it was kind of a wash.

Nowadays, with the advances in technology, we expect more from our low-cal snacks. And though a few good contenders are out there with lots of taste and few calories, they are *very* rare.

I think nutrition bars are among the worst offenders. No matter how many promises the packaging makes—"new and improved," "candy bar taste"—most still taste like a chocolate-covered multivitamin. More often than not, they leave a chalky aftertaste that leaves me feeling like Tom Hanks in the movie *Big* when he bites into a cracker at a party, only to discover it was topped with fish eggs. Gagging, he wipes his traumatized tongue with a napkin.

Let's take a hard look at protein shakes, another taste bud offender. I recently tried a mocha-flavored shake that tasted like a blend of kidneys and cod liver oil with a hint of chicory. It left me wondering if the employees of the food testing kitchen came back after a long Christmas vacation and said, "Let's see what's left in the fridge and make a shake."

Although we now have a large selection of foods and candies sweetened with nonsugar substances, there's usually a tradeoff. Remember Grampaw warning, "Ya don't git somethin' for nothin', honey!" For example, overindulging in certain sugar substitutes will bring a literal meaning to the phrase "puttering around the house."

Entire Web sites extol the deadly ills of certain sweeteners—their originators are certain that Money-Grubbing Cads are behind the proliferation of these substances in every soft drink and snack. Even so, many of us chow down and drink up. When it comes to choosing between developing chronic fatigue syndrome and chronic fat syndrome, we'll take our chances with chronic fatigue any day. Most of us with children already suffer a mommy version of this, anyway.

So until the good Lord returns, I'm convinced our sugar-loving society will keep hope alive that one day someone will discover a sugar substitute that won't leave us bloated, jittery, and cranky. Or, worst of all, puttering around the house with our unwanted pounds in tow.

To me, it's a kind of living metaphor for Christians living in a fallen world. We keep hoping and longing for things in this life to make us truly fulfilled, but each pleasure or venture only satisfies so far and lasts just so long. In our weaker moments, we get frustrated and long for a taste of something that will truly satisfy our souls. In our stronger moments, we understand that the tension we feel is a reflection of the truth that we really weren't designed to be on this planet forever. All roads lead to a future life in a heavenly city where no disappointing substitutes will leave us feeling cheated. Our cravings for the Real Thing will be satisfied once and for all.

The creation waits in eager expectation for the children of God to be revealed. . .in hope that the creation itself will be liberated from its bondage to decay and brought into the freedom and glory of the children of God. . . .We ourselves. . .wait eagerly for our adoption to sonship, the redemption of our bodies.
Romans 8:19–21, 23

Chapter 8

WAKE UP AND SMELL THE BABY
Babies and Disillusionment

Before my first child was born, I remember older, wiser women saying things like, "Enjoy the time you have to yourself before that baby comes!"

At the time, I wasn't thrilled with the time on my hands due to the weight on my bod and the anticipation of seeing the baby in person. I couldn't wait to play dress-up with my real live baby doll. Diaper and formula commercials sent me into la-la land, daydreaming about holding my bundle of joy. I especially liked the ones in which a buff-bodied daddy peeks into Junior's crib in the middle of the night, picks up a porcelain-skinned baby, and nuzzles him. (Notice how the babies are either sleeping or smiling in these propaganda pieces.) I know that's what I had in mind—a studly husband and a picture-perfect baby bonding at 2:00 a.m. in the Ralph Lauren designer nursery while I'm sawing logs in the next room.

But my daydream images became fuzzy with the arrival of baby and the relentless longing for a few hours of uninterrupted shut-eye. My cowardly friends who went before me to baby boot camp didn't clue me in to reality, and I wanted to wring their necks. I ended up not only with a newborn who never slept but also with engorged breasts, each the size of a Goodyear blimp. This turned out to be doubly bad news when I heard the lactation specialist's declaration: "Now remember, the baby's stomach is about the size of an avocado seed." From the looks of things, my baby would need a tummy roughly the size of a water tower to give me even a smidgen of relief.

And what of hubby turned new dad? Well, he discovered talents he never knew he had. He had the uncanny ability to sleep through our baby's cries. So while *he* sawed the logs *I* could only dream about, I cradled my gargantuan mammary glands in my arms and waddled down the hall to the Walmart-decorated nursery, bonding with Junior at 2:00 a.m…and 3:00 a.m. …and 4:00 a.m. I did enough bonding that first year to be the prototype for human superglue.

And I would love to know where the television producers found that porcelain-skinned infant. I quickly became acquainted with the oxymoron "baby acne."

My newborn would have been a shoo-in for a Clearasil commercial. I was so self-conscious about it that I made excuses to strangers in line at the grocery store. "Yes, I try to keep him away from colas, chocolate, and potato chips, but you know how newborns are. . . ."

If you're a mom, I'm preaching to the parental choir. First comes love, then comes marriage, and on the heels of the baby carriage comes disillusionment. Of course, we do experience precious moments with our babies that we will forever hold dear. But on the whole, children are needy and can wreak havoc on your housekeeping, sleep quota, and love life.

When we're knee-deep in diapers, it's important to put things into perspective by reviewing two facts. Fact #1: This is an intense time of life. Fact #2: Babies grow up quickly, and as they do, things get easier. These are time-tested truths—just ask any mother with older children. If you're a relatively new mom or know someone who is and have had a particularly exhausting day (or week or month!), ask God to help you put things in perspective. He may just help you see that beneath your exhaustion is still a heart brimming with gratitude for the priceless, albeit tiring, gift of children.

Children are a heritage from the Lord,

offspring a reward from him.

Psalm 127:3

Chapter 9

NITRO BABIES
Navigating Life's Little Land Mines

Urban legend says the great contortionist Harry Houdini was trained by a mother of tiny tots. After all, who else could hold open a three-hundred-pound glass door with her big toe, force a double stroller through the opening, balance a screaming toddler on her hip, and still retrieve the car keys from her handbag with her teeth? Yet if the truth were told, some of a woman's best contortion maneuvers come into play at naptime.

In quest of the elusive nap, most moms have gone through the equivalent of twelve verses of "Froggie Went a-Courtin'," used up half a gallon of formula, and rocked long enough to unseat Elvis from his throne. The result? We repeatedly nod off into oblivion, while that wide-eyed charge is, well...still charged. Then much later than we would have dreamed (and how we long to dream), we feel the tiny, taut body suddenly give in and go limp. Victory at last! But victory is short-lived because there's still the trek from the rocking chair to the crib.

This precarious task reminds me of the classic Western television show in which a cowboy transports hundreds of vials of highly explosive nitroglycerin in a horse-drawn wagon. The sweaty steed goes *bumpity-bump* over miles of rugged terrain and inevitably encounters a rattlesnake. The camera zooms in on the horse's terror-filled eyes as it rears up on hind legs. Perspiration trickles down the driver's leathery face while the rattlesnake almost cooks his goose.

Now, so close to victory, we Sleep Seekers feel much like that nitro driver. We move like old women, not breathing, sweating profusely, slowly rising from the seat of the rocker. *Whew! So far, so good!* We mentally pat ourselves on the back as we glide carefully to the crib.

Then with the slow-motion precision of a construction crane, we hoist the sleeping bundle over the rail and into position on the mattress. *Now if I can only get my arm out from under his head, I'm home free,* we coach ourselves. As we prepare to let go of baby, we face a technique choice: the Band-Aid removal method (extract your arm at lightning speed) or the

Bomb Squad removal method (extract your arm in painstaking half-inch increments). Regardless of which method we choose, we spy the pacifier lying nearby and note to nab it in the event of a waking emergency. Once our arm is free, we lay the blanket over the baby with stealthy silence. Mission accomplished! And then we step backward to head to our own blissful bed.

Suddenly—*squeak!* We've planted a foot firmly in the midsection of a decidedly unlucky toy ducky lying like a vial of nitroglycerin on the floor. Heart stops. Time stands still. Baby stirs. We frantically leap toward the pacifier and, near tears, softly sing the thirteenth verse of "Froggie went a-courtin' and he did ride, mm-hmm. . . ."

Often life's challenges are like dealing with an insomniac baby. We go through all kinds of uncomfortable internal and external contortions trying to bring peace and rest to situations that wear us thin.

Then, despite our efforts to get things under control, we step on a squeaking duck or, worse yet, on a "vial of nitro" (those doggone emotional land mines). The pitfalls of life are unavoidable. Yet if we become as a little child and call out to God, He will gather us into His arms and still our souls.

Surely I have composed and quieted my soul;
like a weaned child rests against his mother,
my soul is like a weaned child within me.

PSALM 131:2 NASB

Chapter 10

LIVING LARGE

Women's Bodies—One Size Doesn't Fit All

I love big women. Before you get nervous, let me explain. . . .

In Texas, almost every woman drives either an SUV or a van. While I was sitting at an outdoor café, a huge black SUV whipped into the parking lot. The driver was the kind of woman I have admired from afar for years. She filled the driver's compartment with ease and appeared to be about the size of a high school quarterback. Nice, sturdy arms; pretty blond shoulder-length hair; attractive, happy face. She hopped out of her girl-truck, cell phone in hand, flashing white teeth in a smile as big as her SUV. She wore a loose-fitting T-shirt embossed with a Baylor University alumni logo. With confident strides of her sturdy legs, she headed into the café and ordered a Chocolate Java Joe, no apology offered.

Whenever I see this kind of woman, I always feel a twinge of envy and a smidgen of admiration. Women like this seem so doggone. . .*carefree*. Often these women seem to give more bear hugs, laugh with more gusto, and face life with more of a come-what-may attitude. You gotta love 'em!

I think my feelings stem from the fact that these women appear to be comfortable with who they are and with the size of their bodies. It's a rather maverick stance—flying in the face of what society says a beautiful and content woman should look like. Our physically obsessed culture relentlessly flaunts waif-like *young* women with pouty lips and sullen faces as examples of femininity. The politically correct diet of the sexy American woman, according to the Beautiful People, should include bouillon cubes, celery sticks, soy milk, and tofu. Every *truly* health-conscious, beautiful wannabe, the magazines tell us, would spend all of her spare time at the gym with her personal trainer. Often, the truth be told, many gorgeous women (by society's standards) get stuck on the insidious gerbil wheel of always running after but never reaching that "ideal."

Now, if I were twenty years old, parts of this recipe for the "perfect woman" would be appealing. But add another twenty years, extra pounds from three pregnancies, and carting around the fruit thereof on one hip all day, and, well, I'm looking for the recipe for the "real woman." And I think ample women who are living large and happy have at least part of the secret to the recipe.

It occurred to me that God tends to use a lot of creative license. A trip to the zoo quickly demonstrates my point. He made everything from an awkward, leggy pink flamingo to an embarrassing-but-fascinating red-and-blue-bottomed mandrill. As a society, we seem okay with God's creative genius when it involves a variety of personalities—but we can be less accepting when it comes to different kinds of bodies and facial features.

Perhaps you, too, have felt small inside when bombarded with images of what a beautiful woman should look like. As Christian women, we can help each other by shifting our values and focus away from the external and onto the internal—and better yet, to the *eternal*. Let's do our best, with God's help, to make each other feel comfortable and free—accepted for who we are *today*, not some ideal we hope to achieve *someday*. We each must make our own recipe for what the "real me" should look and feel like. But we can leave out that heaping cup of unrealistic expectations.

*I have learned the secret of being content in any
and every situation, whether well fed or hungry.*

PHILIPPIANS 4:12

Chapter 11

THE COLOR PURPLE
Dealing with Dashed Expectations

My three-year-old daughter, Tori, is infatuated with a megastar—a one-name celebrity on a level with Sting, Prince, and Eminem. Recently, upon hearing that the phenom was coming to our city, my friend Katherine and I chaperoned her three-year-old Bayley and my Tori to a live performance. We took the girls to see the heartthrob of the baby set—none other than that prehistoric purple wonder, that dynamite dinosaur himself, the one, the only...*Barney!*

We swallowed hard and forked over thirty dollars per ticket, and yes, the kiddies' tickets were full price! The parking attendant hit us up for another ten dollars, so even before entering the coliseum doors, Katherine and I each had invested a cool sixty-five bucks in this little outing. It had better be good.

Inside the auditorium, the kinetic kiddie energy

almost overwhelmed us. The little tikes clutched their best concert-going paraphernalia: Barney plastic flashlights, Barney baseball hats, Barney T-shirts, etc. The marketers had managed to satisfy kids' every whim while emptying their parents' wallets.

Carefully stepping through the throngs of pint-sized patrons of the purple arts, we found our seats and settled in for the show. Bayley sat in her mom's lap, and Tori sat in mine. The girls chattered happily, and moments later, a male voice boomed over the speaker system, "Ladies and gentlemen! The moment we've all been waiting for: *Barney the dinosaur!*"

The crowd went wild, squealing with delight and raising lighted Barney flashlights high in the darkened auditorium like a zillion points of purple light.

Amid the excitement, I gave Katherine a smug wink. Yep, this is what we paid a small fortune to see—childlike wonder at its commercial best. But before I had even finished my victory wink, Bayley went to pieces. She threw her arms around Katherine's neck and wailed, "Take me hooooome!"

My eyes met Katherine's, and she weakly smiled. The whole scene was too chaotic to ask her what she was going to do, so I concentrated on my own starstruck munchkin, who was begging to be taken onstage.

"I need to give Barney a hug, Mommy!" she explained earnestly.

When the show started, the noise level dropped dramatically, and Bayley became engaged with the action. At the appropriate moments, she sang her previously terrified little heart out. After the show, I asked Katherine what she would have done if Bayley *hadn't* gotten with the program.

"I have to admit, my first thought was to tell that little drama queen I'd just spent sixty-five smackers on this show, and she was gonna like it or else! But it suddenly dawned on me that she wasn't scared of Barney but of the darkness and noise. So I just cuddled her closer and reassured her. When she realized I wouldn't abandon her to the mayhem, she relaxed and enjoyed the show."

Sounds so simple, right? But have *you* ever invested heavily in something only to find it overwhelming? Maybe you prayed for a business, or a ministry, or a family! Even though new experiences can be exciting, sometimes they can seem chaotic and daunting. At times like that, remember: If you've asked God for this challenge, He's the director. He can handle it. Abandon your fear, sit back and relax, let your eyes adjust to the dark, and ultimately enjoy the show with Him. Are you ready? Lights out! Curtains up! Here's the moment you've been waiting for. . .and it's no purple dinosaur!

God has said, "Never will I leave you; never will
I forsake you." So we say with confidence,
"The Lord is my helper; I will not be afraid."
HEBREWS 13:5–6

Chapter 12

ROOT FOR ME
When in Pain, Ask for Help

My visit with my sister at her timeshare had been relaxing and refreshing. The moonlight on the lake below promised a lifetime of tranquility. I sipped from a piping hot mug of green tea and prepared to let out a great sigh: "Ah–h–h–h. . ." What came out of my mouth instead was a wrenching "Argh–h–h!" My right back molar suddenly felt like a miniature volcano preparing to explode.

"Musta been the tea," I muttered and headed for bed, hoping the throbbing would subside. By 3:00 a.m., my tooth had developed the attitude of a cranky New York cabbie.

"Hey!" I could almost hear it. "I'm dyin' he-yah! Can I get some drugs, or *what!*" I scurried to the bathroom and rifled through my overnight bag. I could only find a sample bottle of infant pain-reliever. I unscrewed the top of the one-inch-tall bottle and guzzled the contents like a two-bit junkie—New York–style. As I dragged back to bed, my gaze fell on my teething six-month-old, sleeping peacefully in her port-a-crib.

"Sorry, kid," I whispered apologetically.

After a few more pain-filled days and fitful nights, my toothache morphed into jaw spasm, of all things! It equaled any pain I had ever experienced in childbirth.

What's going on? I wondered as I tried to massage my muscles into submission. *Is it stress? TMJ? What if I have to live with chronic pain for the rest of my life?* My mind raced and my mood deteriorated, while my jaws clenched tighter.

I finally called an acquaintance who was a dentist. "Might be an abscessed tooth," she said. "Call my husband at his oral surgery office. See what he says."

Dr. Pollack examined my jaws and ruled out TMJ. "You should see an endodontist right away," he advised, "but meanwhile, I'm going to give you some strong drugs."

While he wrote the prescription, I sat there looking like Lizard Woman—bulging eyes red and swollen, half shut from sleep deprivation and crying.

After a deliciously restful night of sleep (go drugs!), I went to see the endodontist, Dr. Rakusin. He was a native of South Africa with a lilting accent and soothing voice—a definite plus for someone who is about to yank the roots out from under your tooth. The good doctor, who quickly determined that he faced the equivalent of an agitated Sasquatch, wasted no time getting to the numbing process.

"You will feel a pinch," he said softly as he guided the silver syringe to the roof of my aching mouth. "This might be a little uncomfortable," he added as he poked another spot. I was nervous, but as the pain subsided, I relaxed. For the first time in several days, I felt my lizardness melting away as vestiges of my former self returned.

Then I heard a *whir*, a *clink*, and a *whiz*, and. . .it was over. "That's it?" I asked, incredulous yet grateful.

"That's it!" responded Super Endodontist Man. As he turned to put away his tools, his white coat flung open, and I'm certain I saw a giant *E* emblazoned across his chest. My hee-ro.

In a subsequent visit, the kind doctor dubbed me the endodontist's evangelist. Guilty as charged, I found myself talking to anyone within earshot about the joys of root canals. I was the latter-day Lazarus of dental patients, risen from the abyss of abscess.

When we're hurting, it's easy for our mood to

escalate from troubled to traumatized. If you're going through a tough time emotionally, physically, or spiritually, don't wait for your situation to go from bad to worse. Seek help and encouragement early—whether from a friend or a professional. You may be surprised at how simple (or relatively painless!) the solution might be or how much better you will feel by seeking solace.

"Ask and it will be given to you; seek and you will find; knock and the door will be opened to you."
MATTHEW 7:7

Chapter 13

NOT SO COOL AT STARBUCKS
When Life's Choices Overwhelm You

My preteen son recently discovered the "cool factor" of pricey coffee drinks. Since he doesn't have green hair or a pierced appendage and, more importantly, will still be seen in public with his mother, I've decided to humor him. So every Wednesday morning, we have a date at our neighborhood Starbucks, where Trevor orders a cappuccino with thick froth ("dry"), and I order an oxymoron: a small "tall" cup of coffee. Now I'm the kind of gal who says what she means, so no matter how many times I order, I apologize to the cashier that although I said tall, I *meant* small.

One morning, my non-coffee-drinking hubby filled in for me and escorted Trevor to the coffee bar. At the counter, Trevor ordered his usual—and with flair.

"I'd like a tall mocha cappuccino *dry*, please."

Scott, who was scanning the headlines in the newspaper rack, looked up at Trevor and said, "*Tall?* I think not!" He then directed his next comment to Gidget Goes Barista. "A small will be plenty."

"Sir, a tall *is* a small," she replied, flashing teeth as white as coconut. Trevor quietly slinked behind his father as if trying to disappear. Definitely not a cool situation. The following week, Trevor made double-shot sure I would be free on our "coffee morning."

Okay, enough picking on my not-so-cool husband. Now it's time to pick on me. I had the brainy idea of trying to find a "healthy" drink that would taste like a Frappucino but sans the dairy and sugar. The good news is that I found it. The bad news is that its name contains six words, each integral to ordering the drink I want. That wouldn't be such a big deal if we were talking about a ninety-nine-cent cup o' joe. But when we are talking almost four bucks, it matters that I get it right: iced-decaf-sugar-free-vanilla-soy-latte. It may be easy to say in leisure, but try to say it under pressure!

Some days later, after a shopping excursion, my mom and I stopped at Starbucks to enjoy a drink together. Mom said she wanted to try a warm variation of my drink: decaf-vanilla-soy-latte. Easy enough. Just four little words for her drink and six little words for mine.

But as I approached the counter, the words began to bubble and brew in my brain, and I became hopelessly confused. My palms started to sweat, and I felt like a coffee novice. *How hard can this be? Get it together!* I coaxed myself. But my mind was wet coffee grounds. *What if I forget to say soy and wolf down milk instead— nullifying my week fast from dairy products? What if I forget to say decaf and send Mom's heart rate skipping?*

Fortunately, an experienced barista took pity on me as I stammered the words. Like a kind nurse quelling the pre-op jitters of her petrified patient, she gently assured, "Honey, you can do this. I help people all the time. Trust me—you'll get it right."

The pressure off, I took a deep breath and slowly placed my order—correctly. At least I *think* I got it right. Mom was bouncing off the walls that evening during a game of charades, and it's hard to know if she was reacting to the coffee or just trying to show the kids that Grannie's still "got it."

Choices. If we Americans have anything, it's choices. Some are small (or small tall), some are grande, and some are venti. Wouldn't it be helpful if we always knew the difference and could predict the impact of those choices on our lives? But too many choices at pivotal points in life can leave us feeling like a confused coffee nerd—mouth hanging open at the Starbucks counter. Frozen in time, we may wonder, *What do I do* now? What if I make a mistake and place the wrong order? What if I make a fool of myself? At those times we need to take a deep breath, put our hand in God's, and follow His lead. And like that benevolent barista, He just might say, "You can do this. I help people all the time. Trust Me; you'll get it right!"

Jesus looked at them and said, "With man this is impossible,
but with God all things are possible."
MATTHEW 19:26

Chapter 14

WHITE SHORTS, MOXIE, AND FAITH
Elbowing God Out of the Picture?

If you picked up this book because you consider yourself unconventional, then you may also be a trailblazer in your own right. But here's the real test: How often do you think, *Where there's a will, there's a way?* Yup, we path forgers have a knack for making things happen!

When I was about five years old, white shorts were "in" with girls my age, and I had my eyes on a milky pair I had seen at Ben Franklin's Five and Dime. But Mother explained that white shorts would show dirt, and she'd rather I stick with denim. I remember thinking, *How can she deny me the one piece of clothing that would ensure my lifetime of happiness?*

Looking back, I can't blame Mom. I was a tomboy and spent my summer afternoons playing in the wax-leaf legustrum bushes, where I made a secret bakery hideout. In my little Hole-in-the-Bush Patisserie, I created the most mouthwatering mud pies and drop cookies you ever laid eyes on. During the rainy spring, on my days off from the bakery, I sat curbside and fished bare-handed for fat, pink worms in the rainwater that ran along the curb. In hindsight, I better understand Mom's point of view.

But this is now, and the white shorts were then, and my emerging unconventional will began cooking up a creative alternative to get what I wanted. So I asked Mom for one of Dad's old white T-shirts. She gladly handed over the booty and never questioned my intent.

Later that afternoon, Mom found me playing in the front yard with my buddies—in white shorts. Only they weren't the pair I had seen at Ben Franklin's. I had cut off the bottom portion of my dad's T-shirt, turned the shirt upside down, and slipped my legs through the armholes. I then managed to make the waist fit by tying the excess material in a knot at my waist, and ta-da! Homemade white shorts. Okay, so there was a tiny design flaw— the T-shirt neck opening was not too well hidden in the space between my legs. But I couldn't have been prouder of my makeshift droopy drawers, looking like Mowgli the Jungle Boy. Strangely, Mom didn't share my enthusiasm for the new wardrobe addition. She made a beeline for Ben Franklin's the following morning, and all was right with Mom's world and mine. Sometimes desperate times call for desperate measures, right?

Often when we find ourselves in tough spots, we unconventional ladies get innovative. That may mean making do with what we have until the Lord sees fit to give us what we think will ensure our happiness. It could also mean that as we trust Him to be our Leader, we might find that God has some unconventional ideas of His own about how to best meet our needs.

So, Women of Moxie, when we *really* want something to happen, let's try not to elbow God out of the picture. We unconventional gals need to stick together and help each other stay out of God's way!

TRUST IN THE LORD WITH ALL YOUR HEART AND LEAN NOT ON YOUR OWN UNDERSTANDING; IN ALL YOUR WAYS SUBMIT TO HIM, AND HE WILL MAKE YOUR PATHS STRAIGHT.
PROVERBS 3:5–6

Chapter 15

FRIENDS TO THE FRIENDLESS
Reaching Out to New "Kids" on the Block

During the "Wake Up Crying" time in our family, when we had low dough, an unexpected baby on board, and a move to another state, I struggled to adjust to my new life. I gave myself a good talking-to. "Self," I said, "so you've had a run of tough luck. Enough! Get out and meet some people." So I signed up for a Bible study.

The first study was to be held in a home with brunch following. Sounded like a great idea to me—nothing like bolstering my faith and making new friends over chicken salad and Bundt cake.

So on the morning of the Bible study, I slipped on my $19.99 red maternity jumper, told the roaches to stay off my counters, and drove off in my two-door coupe. After about twenty minutes, miniature mansions surrounded me. *This can't be right,* I thought. *Surely I've made a wrong turn.* But then I spotted a line of shiny

SUVs parked in front of one mansion. A throng of Kathy Lee clones strolled to the entrance between matching topiaries. Feeling like I was about to go fishing for friends in a pond waaaay out of my league, I took a deep breath and mustered up the courage to go inside.

The teacher greeted me at the door and introduced me as a visitor. When the study was over and brunch began, the Kathy Lees metamorphosed into Chatty Kathies—to everybody but me. If I hadn't been hormonal and homesick for my familiar friends, I would have tried initiating small talk. Instead, feeling like a backward schoolgirl in a sea of socialites, I slipped out and drove home—wishing God had made windshield wipers for human eyes.

The following week, the study was, mercifully, held at the church. When I slipped in, the study had already begun, so I sat in the back row by two women I hadn't seen at the brunch. They welcomed me with kind eyes and warm smiles. Soon the duo began whispering wisecracks based on a humorous interpretation of the lesson—just loud enough for the three of us to hear. I gave in to temptation and whispered a funny myself. They giggled softly, flashed those sweet smiles—and I was in like flint.

Nancy Wirth and Cheri Berry befriended this

pregnant foreigner in a strange land. When I was embarrassed to invite them over to my apartment after the baby was born, Cheri sent me this e-mail about her own past housing woes:

> We had enough money to rent a quaint, three-bedroom Victorian. That was the end of the good news. It needed paint inside and out, and the walls were holey with termite damage. The neighbor to our left was an unhappy mother of three who eventually left her husband. She later told us, "When I compared my marriage to yours, I just had to leave." Great, so in addition to wreaking havoc in our own lives, we had managed to spread the wealth like a stomach virus through a preschool. The neighbors to our right had a Doberman that barked at the moon at the stroke of midnight.

After reading that, I complained about my apartment less. At least it was newly painted and termite free!

Interesting, isn't it? Nothing is quite as comforting as talking with someone who's walked a mile in your high heels and completed the journey with her faith (and sense of humor) intact. If you're in dire need of "been there" encouragement, look to a Bible study or support group. If you've survived some Dark Ages of your own, extend a warm welcome to the "strangers among us," and welcome new faces when they appear in your own familiar crowd.

Let brotherly love continue. Be not forgetful
to entertain strangers: for thereby some
have entertained angels unawares.
HEBREWS 13:1–2 KJV

Chapter 16

SEX AND THE HARRIED WOMAN
Where There's a Will, There's a Way

Okay, all you unconventional babes, be honest: You flipped to this page first, didn't you? Well, good for you. At least you have your priorities straight. With the divorce rate running about 50 percent in this nation for both Christians and non-Christians, maybe it's time we hear a little more about this touchy topic.

I'm no Dr. Ruth, and I'm certainly no J.Lo or Demi—although mercifully, when the lights are low, my husband can't seem to tell the difference. Thank God, I don't live in Alaska during the summers when the "midnight sun" lights up the evening sky. Otherwise, I would have to insist that Scott have his eyes dilated prior to entering our Igloo of Love and make him leave his giant sunglasses at the door. If his sight performed at optimum levels, I'm certain he would take one look at me and shout, "Thar she blows!" Next thing you know, I'd be off to have emergency liposuction, providing enough blubber to light the lamps of an entire Eskimo village.

So I'll warn you up front, I'm not doling out personal trade secrets here. You can get all of those you want from a zillion books, including those by Christian authors such as *A Celebration of Sex* (Dr. Douglas Rosenau), *Intimate Issues* (Dillow and Pintus), and *Is There Really Sex After Kids?* (Jill Savage).

I want to share something with you that you probably already suspect but sometimes want to avoid admitting: God wants Christian women to make sex a priority in our marriages. Please understand that I don't think God is asking us to "go through the motions" because it's the right thing to do. I believe He wants us to find out what helps keep the flame of our passion lit rather than let it burn out completely.

What? I hear you wail with exhaustion. *You don't understand! I'm so tired. I help my son deliver his newspaper route at 4:00 a.m., then strap on a harness and tackle my laundry pile, and my whiny kids sap every ounce of energy I have left at the end of the day.*

I hear you, I really do. I, too, climb the summit of Mt. Laundry every day, and I can't remember my last uninterrupted night of sleep, thanks to baby Whitney. But if we hide behind excuses too long, we may find our marriages on shaky ground—which will only add to the list of stress factors in our lives!

Secular author Vicki Iovine cuts to the chase on this topic in her book *The Girlfriend's Guide to Getting Her Groove Back*. The following is my quirky interpretation of her best advice in a nutshell:

1. The Nike Approach—just do it!
2. The Dress for Success Method—suit up and show up!
3. The Martha Stewart Method—repeat to yourself, "Sex is a good thing."

So if you struggle with this area of your life, consider exploring ways to find victory. In our sexually charged culture, Christian wives need to go on the offensive. This may mean making peace with the occasionally confusing duality of our spirituality and sexuality. It may mean seeing a therapist to be set free from sexual hang-ups and misconceptions. Be willing to do whatever it takes to rejoice in the hottie of your youth (to paraphrase the king of biblical hotties—Solomon, the sensual songwriter).

Okay, Wild Thang, you can read the rest of the book now.

The wife does not have authority over her own body but yields it to her husband. In the same way, the husband does not have authority over his own body but yields it to his wife.
1 CORINTHIANS 7:4

Chapter 17

MERRY DAIRY
Your Way or the Highway?

Only the doctor's hands are visible on the TV screen, unwrapping the gauze from a woman's face and head. Now we hear his solemn voice: "I'm so sorry. . .so sorry. The operation was not a success."

Still we have not seen the woman's face. We only see her hands as the doctor places a mirror in them. The woman screams, and the camera focuses on her face. We see that she is. . .drop-dead gorgeous! The camera then pans the room to reveal the faces of the doctor and nurses—who all have hideous pig faces. Welcome to the *Twilight Zone* television series, circa 1950.

I felt like the woman in that spellbinding episode as our family spilled out of our van at the Merry Dairy in a small town. Why had we chosen to take a vacation in the dead of summer with two babies and a preteen and his buddy? Parental tension rose with the mercury until my husband decided it was time for soft-serve therapy.

My anticipation of a cool cone was immediately tempered as I opened the glass door and stepped onto the welcome mat. The mat looked like it had a night job as an oil change mat at the local Fasty Lube. Suddenly, I wasn't feeling so merry and began to lose my appetite for dairy. I excused myself to the Little Dairy Maids' Room and was not reassured. A cook's apron hanging on the back of the door had bits of raw hamburger attached, attracting a trio of flies.

Oh yeah, I thought sarcastically, *that will perk up my appetite.* I exited as quickly as I could but couldn't shake the feeling that I had entered the twilight zone of ice cream/burger joints.

I spotted my family happily licking dip cones amid booths of locals. Then I spied an older, unkempt gentleman who was smiling and approaching baby Whitney. She flirted shamelessly, beaming at him from my husband's arms. I shot to her faster than a speeding bullet, noticing the man's arm—tattooed with a naked lady, drawn in striking anatomical detail. The smell of liquor emanated from where the man's front teeth had once been.

"Wow!" I said, boring my eyes into my husband's

and faking a smile. "Would you look at the time? Come on, kids, head 'em up and move 'em out!"

Safely back in the van (it now seemed like a haven, so our mission was accomplished in an odd way), I tried to figure out why the locals frequented this establishment. It was clearly a hangout—albeit for the down-and-out. I wondered, *Can't they see how gross the place is? Why do they have such low standards for cleanliness?* I could only figure that, like the woman in the *Twilight Zone* show, they judged things by a different standard—and were satisfied. And you know what? I should be okay with that.

A mentor once told me that we basically see life through one perspective—our own. Yet seeing things from another's perspective can make us wiser and empathetic. The next time we feel stuck in the twilight zone way of seeing something, we may want to ask God if He has something important for us to see before we rush to judge.

WE PUT UP WITH ANYTHING RATHER THAN HINDER THE GOSPEL OF CHRIST.
1 CORINTHIANS 9:12

Chapter 18

BIG KID
Making Memories for Little Kids

After only a few dates, I sensed something was different about Scott. While we were still in the getting-to-know-you stage, he took me to an ice cream parlor owned by a former figure skater (yeah, I know—go figure). We hopped onto pink revolving stools at Sow Cow Scoops, and Scott asked, "Whatcha gonna get?" In those days, I had a recognizable waistline to watch, so I answered, "How about a scoop of vanilla?"

"Va-NIL-a?" he shot back with a pitiful frown. "Come on, live a little. Wouldn't you really rather have a dip of Double Dark Fudge with Triple Lutz Nuts?"

I thought about it a half second or so. "Now that you mention it, yes, I *would*!"

Later that evening, we went to a concert that was packed with people. I figured we'd be sitting in the nosebleed section where we could only *hear* Amy Grant and see Adam Ant. But Super Sleuthing Activity Director told me to stay near a light pole until his return. Fifteen minutes later, my hee-ro returned. "Let's go! I found a great spot down front," he gloated.

A month later, on one starlit evening near Christmas, Scott sat me down at a table in the open-air market of Merchant's Square in Colonial Williamsburg. "Close your eyes," he instructed. I closed my eyes but strained my ears, hoping to hear the quiet crackling sound of wrapping paper as he placed a beautifully gift-wrapped package in front of me. But alas, all was calm and all was bright (as far as I could tell with my eyes closed), and I couldn't hear much of anything.

"Okay, you can open them now," Scott announced. When I opened my eyelids, there stood Scott, holding a bright red Christmas stocking with the words RACHEL AND SCOTT appliquéd on it. Sounds like a sweet, understated gift to give your new sweetheart, right? But the stocking was so big, all I could see was the tippy-top of Scott's head.

Well, you know how the story ends. I married the Big Kid, who became a television producer, and we began producing babies. At the pinnacle of Scott's career, he worked for the Turner Network in Atlanta. His office building housed TNN, TCM, TBS, and the Cartoon Network. Each network had its own floor, and the décor reflected the programming. Scott used to take our then eight-year-old Trevor and me to see where he worked. We always stopped on the Cartoon Network floor to visit the four-foot-tall gumball machine. Life-sized images of Scooby Doo, Power Puff Girls, and Fred Flintstone stared at us in suspended animation from the walls. Trevor's smile seemed permanent the moment we stepped into the Turner Building, and I was grateful that my little kid had a Big Kid to look up to.

God has shown me that my life is richer because my playful husband is never too far from his own sense of childlike wonder. And he is heaven-bent on sharing the wealth. If you don't have a Big Kid in your life, maybe you should pray for one to come along—or better yet, ask God to help you become one by reconnecting with your childlike sense of wonder.

And he said: "Truly I tell you, unless you change and become like little children, you will never enter the kingdom of heaven."
MATTHEW 18:3

Chapter 19

SUPERMARKET LOYALTY
Looking Out for Number One

So what do you think about the new "Preferred Customer" card at your local supermarket? The first one at the first store kinda makes you feel among the elite, right? Card-carrying shoppers are treated to two-for-one rutabagas and a free bottle of children's vitamins with every purchase of Sugar Poofs cereal— the antidote right along with the poison. Such a deal, dahling! One locally owned store in our small town has upped the ante in the War for Regulars with the guilt-inducing tactic of designating their cards "Loyalty Cards."

Well, I wanted to be loyal, but I soon found every other supermarket in town was also giving out preferred customer cards—and I took them all. In my fleeting moments of rock-solid self-assertion, it doesn't bother me that my Brookstone Loyalty Card lies within my purse, nestled in a stack of a dozen or so preferred customer cards. Yet in my weaker moments of irrational empathy, I feel I am a Grocery Adulteress. How can I live with myself when I shun the down-home smiles and "Can I hep ya" service of this locally owned store—when I run wantonly into the arms of every grocery store within a ten-mile radius of my house looking for great deals?

The last time I bought groceries at Brookstone's, I squirmed while I checked out. I recognized the handsome, clean-cut checker. Ever chipper and polite, Cody was dressed in a crisp white shirt and black skinny tie and greeted me with a beaming smile.

"Good morning, Mrs. St. John! Do you have your loyalty card today?"

"Why, yes, I do!" I smiled nervously. I began pawing through my billfold for the card from Cody's store. I couldn't put my fingers right on it, so I tried to act nonchalant while blindly searching through my purse. At the same time, I conversed with Nice Tie Guy. After pulling out a gas card, credit card, and movie rental card, I dumped the contents of my purse on the conveyor belt. Picking through my multicolored stack of preferred customer cards, sweating profusely from the shame, I searched wildly for the black one with "Brookstone's" written in red letters. I finally found it.

"See?" I smiled weakly and handed over the prized piece of plastic. "I told you I had it."

Cody looked pained, while I gathered my lipstick, pens, and a couple of pink pouches of feminine pads from the conveyor belt. He said not a word. He didn't have to. I felt so cheap.

Loyalty can be hard to give, especially when we make decisions based upon self-interest—when we don't consider the impact on our relationships with others and with God. If our loyalty is divided between the enticing "deals" this world offers and what God offers, we may squirm when He asks to see our Spiritual Loyalty Card.

May our desire to honor Him outweigh the pull of the world. And may the Grocery Bag of Our Lives be filled with words and deeds that reflect a heart loyal to Him.

"'Love the Lord your God with all your heart
and with all your soul and with all your mind.'
This is the first and greatest commandment."
Matthew 22:37–38

Chapter 20

CREATIVE SAVANTS
Munchkins, Messes, and Meaning

This morning my three-year-old daughter had a bad case of what I call "toddler PMS." Tori's sensitivity alarm was ratcheted up to go off at the touch of a feather. She lodged a series of complaints, each accompanied by wailing, flailing, and falling into a heap on the floor. Her Cheerios were floating on the wrong side in her cereal bowl; I had mistakenly screwed Elmo's head onto Barney's sippy-cup body. And, heaven forbid, I had committed the unpardonable sin of cutting her toast lengthwise rather than diagonally.

I knew we had a long day ahead of us if this continued, so I decided it was time for art therapy—a little trick I picked up by watching movies about crazy people in psych wards. It's amazing the difference a little crayon and paper make. Things immediately looked up. Before long, I was enjoying the peaceful ambiance of classical music drifting from the CD player as I hauled out more sanity-saving supplies: glue, glitter, stickers, markers, and paint. It was all coming out of the craft closet to rescue my morning. I needed quiet time to make phone calls, and I was on my way to professional productivity!

Three calls later, I returned to Tori. She had made a beautiful body of "water," aka Glue Lake, on my kitchen table. She had also covered every square inch of her white kid's table with red marker and, while tracing her hands several times, also had clearly experienced an epiphany. *Hey? Why just trace my hands when I can color them in solid?* Why do preschoolers always think that if a little is good, a lot must be better? Even after a good scrub-down, her fingernails remained a lovely shade of Frankenstein green.

Recently a friend gave me a magnet that reads, "Cleaning House While the Kids Are Young Is Like Shoveling Snow While It's Snowing." We all secretly hope that our little Picassos will be the next Norman (or Norma) Rockwell. How else can we find some sense of purpose in the thousands of hours we spend cleaning up after creative childhood endeavors?

Well, take heart. Steven Spielberg's parents say that, as a baby, he was very hard to get to sleep—and stayed that way. Can I hear an amen from the masses of bedtime-routine-exhausted mommies out there? Later when Steven was a teen, his mother let him fill her pressure cooker with a dozen cans of cherries in heavy syrup to create a special effect for one of his early homemade movies. Mrs. Spielberg said she found cherry bits in her kitchen for the next eight years. And the rest is movie-making history.

So the next time you have to wade through piles of coloring books, buckets of crayons, and globs of glittered glue, remember that God may have a creative genius cooking there. And it may only be another twenty years or so until you find out for sure. But in the meantime, envision yourself at the Oscars or a Pulitzer Prize dinner in a sequined evening dress, hearing your grown-up kid tell the world, "I owe this night to my mom, who taught me how to make something great out of my messes." Until then, pray for patience and invest in a well-organized craft cabinet.

But let patience have her perfect work.
JAMES 1:4 KJV

SURVIVAL OF THE PRETTIEST
Inner Beauty Is More Than Skin Deep

Have you ever noticed that we women would really rather pal around with other women who are equally or even less attractive than we are? It's tough on the ol' ego to feel like the female counterpart of Jerry Lewis hanging out with pretty-boy Dean Martin.

I once dated a guy who had just returned home from a hospital stay. He was living at his parents' house and mentioned that his old girlfriend, who was a friend of the family, was on her way over to say hello.

"Great!" I said with a tight smile. I really wanted to say, "Well, if she wants to be a goodwill ambassador, maybe she should be a candy striper and make her rounds at the hospital instead of your house."

From that moment until "the other woman" arrived, I felt like I was trapped in an out-of-body experience. Although I could hear Brian and his parents talking with me, I was in a daydream-nightmare. I could only think about how I would be dethroned as Brian's girl by a "friend of the family," who was no doubt a soap opera vixen as beautifully sinister as Susan Lucci.

Suddenly, the doorbell rang. As Sheri walked into the den, my heart beat rapidly and I wanted to disappear. She could have been the cover girl for, well, Cover Girl. She was a stunning, fresh-faced natural blond beauty. But upon shifting my focus a little lower, my heart stopped pounding, and I arose from the ashes of my insecurities like the mythical, feather-plucked phoenix—reborn and ready to take flight. The reason? This Britney Spears look-alike had huge hips.

Despite that one small victory, I have had several experiences of playing the homely sidekick to an array of show-stoppingly beautiful women. I can just hear my friends. "Rachel, come on now, you're exaggerating." Well, maybe a little. But in comparison to these hot chicks, I *felt* like a bucktoothed Laura Ingalls Wilder in a homemade flour sack dress. Obviously, my internal tussle with fleeting self-esteem indicated that I am powerfully affected by the prevailing notion that "beautiful is better."

Beautiful women are esteemed as pop icons for us average-looking masses. Interestingly, in some cultures, wisdom is honored over sleek legs and taut tummies; and post-prime women are valued more for their rock-solid character than washboard abs. Even so, I've learned one thing from befriending a few real babes: If a woman is secure in who she is, it doesn't matter if she looks like Julia Roberts or Roseanne Barr—she's a joy to be around. I've also noticed that when I lose myself in conversation with another woman, her face fades into the background, and my focus turns to her eyes and expressions and, most importantly, to her heart.

So why should we sink into the trap of believing that "beautiful is better"? God is busy working on inner countenances that improve with age. Let's remember that we're in this for the long haul. Daughters of the King need never feel inferior or intimidated, so let's keep this in mind and be gracious to knockouts and plain Janes alike.

Daughters of kings are among your honored women. . . .
Let the king be enthralled by your beauty;
honor him, for he is your lord.
PSALM 45:9, 11

CONFESSIONS OF A CARB LOVER
Moderation Is Such a Lonely Word

If you've hit the midlife metabolism slowdown, every morsel you contemplate must face the three-word inquisition: "How many carbs?" I don't know about you, but I am distressed that comfort foods like homemade biscuits and chicken and dumplings are on the McCarthy-esque Blacklist of Commie Foods out to undermine the very fabric of our physiques.

The dreaded carb count has plunged me into the throes of dietary angst more often than I care to admit. How many times have I ached for just one slice of Chocolate Volcano Cake but was restrained by the fact that, instead, I could eat the body weight of a Sumo wrestler in frankfurters for a fraction of the carbo-hydrates. It's the dietary equivalent of turning down a freewheeling motorcycle date with Fonzie for a month of Sunday drives in the family station wagon with Richie Cunningham.

Supposedly the trouble with carbs is that they quickly convert to sugar, and that's a bad thing. Many of us find this hard to fathom. Sugar has been our friend since we devoured that icing-laden cupcake at our first birthday party. Sugar was there for us during the dog days of childhood boredom, helping us while away the hours as we blew bubbles from soft pink gum. And in our teen years, we looked cool by simply nursing a can of sugary Coca-Cola with our peers. And as adults, sugar has been there for us with countless after-dinner pick-me-ups like Gimme Chocolate or Gimme Death Fudge Pie.

So what's a card-carrying carb lover to do? Maybe practice moderation in eating pasta, breads, and sweets. Ouch. I hate that. But I'm not fond of the jigglyness of my tush and thighs when I don't practice moderation. So I'll usually pass on Fonzie Carbs and go steady with Richie Proteins—and still respect myself in the morning.

Moderation sounds like such a grown-up, *boring* concept. But it can be just the ticket for those indulgences in life that can quickly turn into overindulgences. When we struggle with self-discipline and need the *m* word, it's a good idea to ask a friend to help us with prayers and accountability until we have some successes under our belt (perhaps literally). That friend probably has her own short list of temptations and also needs your support and prayer.

Whether you're a carb-lovin' fool or just feel foolish because you can't seem to garner the self-discipline to overcome a temptation, don't forget that God is on your side—waiting to help you cross into victory.

No temptation has overtaken you except what is common to mankind. And God is faithful; he will not let you be tempted beyond what you can bear. But when you are tempted, he will also provide a way out so that you can endure it.
1 Corinthians 10:13

Chapter 23

GANGING UP ON PMS
Manhandling the Monthly Visitor

I don't know about your husband, but around "that time" each month, mine would like me to disappear. Frankly I, too, would like to go away for about a week, preferably at Spas"R"Us. Instead, I pop some Advil and get dinner on the table while baby Whitney whacks my shins with her runaway walker.

I distinctly remember the day I first realized I might have a touch of PMS. It was 1992, and I had loaded baby Trevor for a trip to the mall. Of course, since he was my first baby, I lugged about fifty pounds of paraphernalia including a three-in-one stroller that turned out to be as simple as unfolding a Sherman tank. I felt a little crampy, so I took my sweet time circling the parking lot to find a close spot. Soon I spied one. *Who says God doesn't care about the little things?* I thought, grateful for the break.

As I swung my car to pull into the space, two leather-clad, teenaged motorcycle-riding thugs roared in front of me and into *my* spot—the spot that God had just provided and *ordained* for me and my baby. I was *torqued*.

I rolled down my window and let 'em have it! "You boys need to get some manners!" I yelled. They laughed, and I floored it out of there, leaving skid marks in my wake. Heart pounding, I realized I could have jeopardized my baby's safety and my own. Feeling lower than a louse, I called my sister that evening to confess my irresponsible behavior.

To my surprise, she laughed. And then she unfurled her own PMS confession. "You shoulda been here the day I lobbed a half gallon of milk past my hubby's head and splattered it all over the wall!"

She then referred me to Jean Lush's book *Emotional Phases of a Woman's Life*, which addresses PMS. I found it reassuring that my hormonal outbursts hadn't escalated to the point of spraying Scott in the face with a dangerous substance, as one woman had confessed. But I suspected such a radical response might not be too far away if I didn't figure out how to quell my premenstrual irritation. So I saw my doctor, and he suggested the usual: Back off of caffeine and sugar, get some exercise and rest, and beef up on vitamins B, C, and calcium—and if all else fails, consider anti-anxiety medication. I'm happy to report that ten years down the PMS pike, I have refrained from giving Harley-driving roadies a good spanking. Now, I *do* occasionally get a little irritable when my neatnick husband discusses the virtues of organizing our food closet alphabetically. I just tell him he can take his alphabet and go watch *Sesame Street* while I rifle through the disheveled pantry for a chocolate fix.

It's easy to make fun of PMS, but if you suffer from serious stress and find yourself morphing from Susie Homemaker to Death Row Darla in zero to sixty, you might want to check with your doctor. God loves us and wants us to be at peace with our bodies and spirits, so don't get down on yourself—reach out for help and encouragement. And meanwhile, steer clear of motorcycle gangs.

AS A FATHER HAS COMPASSION ON HIS CHILDREN, SO THE LORD HAS COMPASSION ON THOSE WHO FEAR HIM; FOR HE KNOWS HOW WE ARE FORMED, HE REMEMBERS THAT WE ARE DUST.
PSALM 103:13–14

Chapter 24

SLOTH MOM
Pacing Yourself

I'm a "laid-back" mom by nature. Although that may sound enviable to some supercharged moms, it's not politically correct in today's fast-paced society. For example, my day started out routinely enough like any high-energy gal's would by taking a bath. But once I had a tub full of water and bubbles, and my little one was contentedly watching friendly bilingual dragons, I figured, *Hey, I don't want to waste this hot water, so I'd better soak a bit.*

By the time I dried my hair, put on my makeup, and dressed, an hour had passed. Tori had moved on from *watching* animated dragons to *depicting* them on my kitchen floor. I thought they were dragons, anyway, but to be honest, they resembled roadkill of a marsupial heritage. A bottle of Soft Scrub and a half hour later, I was ready to rock 'n' roll. With to-do list in hand,

I announced to my budding Rembrandt, "Time to go bye-bye in the blue van!" Something about escaping the confines of the house with a preschooler makes me instantly feel productive.

By the time we waited in line at the bank, it was 11:00 a.m. and time to think about lunch. Feeling slightly guilty that my child had not run around much outside due to cold weather, I opted for a dining experience replete with life-sized chutes and ladders. Once there, I chatted with another mom and we decided to go for the gold under the arches and indulge in leisurely, sparkling banter over coffee and dessert (rectangular apple pie, but tasty nonetheless).

The next thing I knew, noon was long gone, and I anxiously noted my list less traveled, our laundry left undone, and meat for dinner still rock solid in the freezer.

I continued to crawl at this snailish pace throughout the afternoon, and as dinnertime rolled around, I wondered again, *Where did the time go? Why didn't I at least get the undies washed and make a dent in the pile of papers cluttering my counter?*

I often feel something akin to a turtle swimming in a barrel of molasses. *Why can't I seem to switch from Park to Drive without a Herculean effort? What's wrong with me?*

I ask while soaking in the tub (this is the *night*time bath).

So I do a little self-loathing and then call my buddy Jane Jarrell, author of *Secrets of a Midlife Mom*, food stylist for *Dallas Morning News*, keynote speaker, wife, mother, rocket scientist—you name it. I call Jane because, honestly, I like to hear how guilty she feels about flying about the country juggling so much exciting work with a husband and little girl in tow. Yes, I make myself feel better by comparing myself to Jane. And you know what? She feels better after talking with me—the human sloth who counts it an accomplishment to thaw a pound of frozen hamburger in any given afternoon.

Are you caught in the trap of comparing your mothering style to someone else's? The grass may not be as green on the other side of the cul-de-sac as it appears. Maybe we would be much better off to ask God to show us the positive aspects of our personality and how those qualities uniquely meet the needs of the children and husband He has entrusted to us. Meanwhile, there's no harm in admiring the style and pace of another mom and even learning a few good tips from her—but we should make sure our admiration doesn't slide into enviable comparison.

We do not dare to classify or compare ourselves.
2 Corinthians 10:12

Chapter 25

OLDY MOLDY
Tossing Out the Garbage of Past Sin

If you're a thirty- to forty-something woman, you may have at least one parent who lived through the Great Depression. My mother was a knobby-kneed, freckled sibling among six others in a small town in West Texas during that hardscrabble time. Her family's economical, starch-based sustenance would have been Dr. Atkins's worst nightmare: biscuits, gravy, bread, and the ubiquitous pinto bean. Since they had no money for toys, necessity became the mother of invention, and Mom spent many happy hours making clothes for homemade paper dolls and searching for old bottles in the "prairie dog field" across the road from their country house.

Mom now lives in a nice home with my dad, who is retired from the aeronautics industry. So I'm surprised when I see reminders of Depression-esque behavior in my upper-middle-class mom. For example, she used to use the cotton stoppers from her vitamin bottles to apply her nightly astringent. "Why waste a perfectly good piece of cotton?" she reasoned. My dad finally stopped that. He didn't want to spoon with a woman who smelled as if she had spritzed herself with Liz Taylor's Passion, then rubbed herself down with a B-12 tablet.

More recently, during one of my mother's visits to my house, I wandered sleepily into the dimly lit guest bathroom one night and was suddenly jolted wide awake. Underneath the vanity was some sort of animal. Fuzzy, dirty, bedraggled. . . I reached for the plumber's friend leaning in a corner and bent low, determined to get him before he got me. Upon closer inspection, relief washed over me. It was only a pair of my mother's once pink, well-worn, highly treasured house slippers.

The next morning when I asked her why she didn't get a new pair, she swore that the current ones were destined for the garbage can as soon as she found a comfortable replacement pair. Yeah, right. It won't surprise me, replacement slippers or not, if I find the Varmint Slippers in some dark corner of her closet when she's gone to be with Jesus. I can see her now, snickering at me from the entrance to the Pearly Gates, as I lie in her closet with a coronary from another run-in with the house slippers that wouldn't die.

The propensity to hold on to things in case the Specter of Want should rear its ugly head once again is rather funny. That philosophy probably holds some wisdom, but it also reminds me of how, in a spiritual sense, we can hang on to our sins way past their freshness date and until they become stale and moldy, threatening to harm our ability to move forward in forgiveness.

Few women aren't at least occasionally plagued by guilt about words spoken and choices made in situations they wish they had handled differently. Sometimes we just can't seem to let our sins go into God's Trash Bin of Forgiveness. Roughly translated, Psalm 103:12 assures believers that God is—figuratively speaking—following us around with a heavy-duty, thirty-gallon trash bag, ever ready to take our unkind words, selfish actions, and every other sin to the Great Landfill of things forgiven and forgotten. Sometimes we need to remember it's time to toss out the old and make a fresh start as new creations in Christ.

As far as the east is from the west,
so far has he removed our transgressions from us.
PSALM 103:12

IS GOD PULLING YOUR LEG?
He Keeps Coming Back for You

Goosey, goosey gander,
Whither shall I wander?
Upstairs and downstairs
And in my lady's chamber.
There I met an old man
Who would not say his prayers.
I took him by the left leg
And threw him down the stairs.

As bizarre and mean-spirited as this sounds, many of us feel God will do that and worse to us if we don't get our spiritual act together. If we're not praying without ceasing, daily reading His Word, or pondering deep thoughts from Yancey and Lucado, we think that God is out to get us. We see God as the Big Boogeyman, lurking around, ready to jump out of the shadows of our lives, grab us by our left leg, and hurl us down a flight of stairs without warning. And as our head bounces off each step, He's calling out, "You deserved that!" So we withdraw from Him in fear, waiting for the other celestial shoe to drop.

On the opposite end of the spectrum, some of us might feel God is so high on grace that He is, in fact, the Cosmic Cool Dude. He hangs out in trendy coffeehouses, sipping latte while relaxing to smooth jazz—virtually unaffected by our bad behavior. And even if we were to trouble Him with the unseemly details, we're sure He'd respond, "No problem."

We wonder, *Could God possibly be that interested in me?* We figure the Pearly Gates probably sport a sign stating, CLOSED DUE TO LACK OF INTEREST. So we continue to do what we please, letting our relationship with Him grow distant and cold.

I rather think God is more like the Leading Man in those wonderful 1940s black-and-white movies. When we make unwise choices and realize how badly our sin has hurt us and others, we may want to lock ourselves in the bedroom of life—whether from fear or avoidance—vowing never to come out again. But our Leading Man stands outside the door, with the quiet strength of a Jimmy Stewart, tapping softly.

"Let's talk about it," He calls. "Open up, please. I just want us to be together. I love you so much."

I'm no biblical scholar, but even I can guarantee that God will not grab you by your left leg and throw you down life's stairwell if you don't get it right in your day-to-day choices. I'm also confident that I'm on solid theological ground when I say God doesn't mind being "bothered" by our confession of sins. He has promised to forgive us and help us to move past failure and on to victory. And I'm *certain* that God would prefer to share our lives with us rather than be locked out because we're afraid of Him or we think He doesn't care enough to get involved.

So when you blow it, remember that God is not interested in throwing you down the stairwell or brushing you off as a nuisance. Instead, in your hour of need for mercy, reach outward and upward for the strong hand and big heart of your Leading Man. Let Him lead you higher—out of the shadows and into the light.

Let us then approach God's throne of grace with confidence, so that we may receive mercy and find grace to help us in our time of need.
Hebrews 4:16

Chapter 27

IF LOOKS COULD KILL
The Green-Eyed Monster

I only had a "hiyah" relationship with Patty, but I noticed her every time I saw her in our relatively small town. In contrast to us football moms who ran errands in jeans and T-shirts, she was always impeccably dressed in tailored suits—her auburn hair bouncing on her shoulders like a shampoo model. Her makeup was ever fresh, and although she wasn't a classic beauty, Patty had appeal. *For Pete's sake,* I felt like saying, *why can't she, like the rest of us, go to Walmart once in a while looking like something the cat dragged home?*

One night after a tough go at putting my kids to bed, then diving right into writing, I looked at the clock and realized it was midnight. It occurred to me that if I didn't run to the store and get some milk, trouble would be brewing alongside my coffee grounds in the morning. Although I've tried, on several milkless occasions, to extol the praises of using orange juice to wet down their cereal, my kids don't buy my "make do" propaganda.

So, looking like a homeless person—T-shirt dotted with teething biscuit slime, blurred eyeliner the only visible trace of makeup left—I decided to head for the grocery store. My hair was as flat and stringy as Cher's—but the look wasn't as attractive on me as it is on her.

"Ah, well," I sighed, heading out the door. "I'll probably be the only customer at this time of night anyway."

At the store, I stared at the paper plate display, trying to decide if I should spring for the cute zoo animal ones, when a woman rolled her cart by me rather hastily. She seemed a bit furtive but offered an obligatory "Hi."

In the split second she passed me, I noticed she wasn't wearing makeup, either, and even had a couple of glowing red zits on her chin. *Good,* I thought, *I'm not the only shameless mommy in this town who is seen in public looking like cat kill.*

And then it hit me. The woman was Perfect Patty. And I thought, *Man! She looks awful! I can't believe she's in public looking like that.* I couldn't have been more pleased. But on the drive home, I wondered, *What does this say about me?* Here I was, looking like I'd hopped off the nearest boxcar, and I'd just pointed the finger at my fellow hobo and declared that my knapsack look was better than hers. Was I envious of Patty's together, hip persona? I think so.

In my heart, I knew that if I got to know Patty, I'd probably find not only that she was nice but also that she struggled with feeling inferior in some area. Then I would be ashamed of myself for envying her. The Bible talks about examining the speck in someone else's eye while we have a log in our own. Or in my case, pointing out the zits on someone else's chin while ignoring the teething biscuit on my own. It's always a good idea to let the scriptures be our "spiritual compact mirror" each day and make sure we are examining our own hearts instead of judging someone else's.

"Resentment kills a fool,
and envy slays the simple."
Job 5:2

Chapter 28

MR. WRONG?
Married the Wrong Guy?

One morning as I was awakening, a startling thought sat me bolt upright in bed. *Oh my goodness! I've married the wrong man!*

I understand this is not a rare phenomenon, especially early in marriage. Some of us make that life-long commitment while we're still young enough to use acne cream. To make matters even more ludicrous, an endorphin-infused "love high" impairs our ability to walk in a straight line, much less think rationally.

In the early days after the honeymoon, we thrive on the "opposites attract" phenomenon. I love eggs, he loves bacon; I love chick flicks, he loves action films; I love to sleep in on Saturdays, he loves to get up early. As time marches on, what intrigued us and was endearing about our mate begins to drive us nuts. Years down the road, all that bacon has given your prince a pot belly. He won't take you to a movie unless the starring role is played by Ahnold, and your luscious Saturday morning sleep-in is rudely interrupted by the crackling whir of the weedeater outside your bedroom window. Charming.

Author John Eldredge describes his own "courtship to marriage" hike and admits getting seriously lost in the deep woods for a time. He writes about the night he fell for his wife:

"We kissed that night, and though I'd kissed a few girls in my time, I had never tasted a kiss like that. Our friendship had turned to love without my really knowing how or why, only that I wanted to be with this woman for the rest of my life." He then adds: "Why was it that ten years later I wondered if I even wanted to be married to her anymore?"

Most of us can say we were not in our right minds when we married. What were we thinking, making a lifelong commitment to another human being at the age of twenty-something?

But more to the point, what was God thinking? Doesn't He consider the folly of youth and its hormone rushes? Probably. I also think God's goal is probably to make us complete and that part of His plan is to use—you guessed it—that charming spouse.

I think we enter marriage looking like a piece of

swiss cheese with lots of emotional holes to fill up, and God often gives our mate many round pieces to fill those holes. But the trick is having two people committed to seeing their relationship through the holey stage. If we hang in there long enough and are both willing to grow, we find that marriage has gone from holey to whole—helping shape us into the people God created us to be. And with the passing years, we find we have become one in heart and mind.

For this cause shall a man leave his father and mother,
and shall be joined unto his wife, and they two shall be one flesh.
This is a great mystery.
EPHESIANS 5:31–32 KJV

Chapter 29

THE SOUND OF MUSIC SURVEY
Friends, Opposites, and Favorite Things

I've heard that friends must have enough common interests to get along well and enough differences to make things interesting. You know the song: "You like tomato and I like tomahto. . . ." That sure is the case with my friend Kimberlyn and me. We're both writers, have preteens, and are unconventional "midlife" moms. She loves quaint. I love quirk. She loves the romantic Victorian era and all things Beatrix Potter. She has even named her house Linden Cottage. I, on the other hand, am more of a "tomboy's woman." I like the distressed look of French Country and all things Sesame Street. I have also named my house: the Nut Haus. Recently I suggested that we see just how different we are in certain areas. So we put on our Julie Andrews thinking caps and, with our best *Sound of Music* savvy, wrote down a few of "our favorite things":

MUSIC
Kimberlyn: Classical, Pachelbel's "Canon in D"
Rachel: Country, "Did I Shave My Legs for This?"

KID'S BEDTIME STORY
Kimberlyn: *The Secret Garden*
Rachel: *Elmo Has a Boo-Boo*

KID'S BIRTHDAY PARTY
Kimberlyn: Tea party at the Ritz-Carlton
Rachel: Mr. Cheesy's Pizza Parlor

BRUNCH SPOT
Kimberlyn: The Blue Owl Tea Room
Rachel: The Donut Palace

BOOK
Kimberlyn: Jane Austen's *Pride and Prejudice*
Rachel: *The Complete Idiot's Guide to Organizing Your Life*

DEVOTIONAL BOOK
Kimberlyn: Oswald Chambers's *My Utmost for His Highest* (in the original, archaic language, of course!)
Rachel: Emilie Barnes's *Fifteen Minutes Alone with God*

Although Kimberlyn has more refined tastes, we enjoy each other's company and have learned a good deal in the process. For example, after talking to her, I realized that my favorite classical piece was in fact called Pachelbel's "Canon" and not Taco Bell's "Canon." And I also learned that the purists do not consider doughnuts a pastry. Kimberlyn says that they are in a food group alone—ditto for pork cracklins. She's learned a few things from me, too. Namely, that "ain't" is the primary compound verb that holds a good country song together and that you can buy a *Complete Idiot's Guide* to just about anything under the sun. She commented, "That title sounds patronizing to me." I replied, "What's *patronizing* mean?"

Isn't it great how friends can expand each other's horizons? Good friends with whom we have much in common—as well as those with many differences—can keep us from getting stuck in a rut, provide a new perspective when we face a tough decision, and help us laugh when we feel like crying. Simply put, friends can double our joy and halve our sorrow.

Why not grab a friend and conduct an informal *Sound of Music* survey of your own? Don't be surprised if one of you bursts into an operatic rendition of "Climb Every Mountain" while the other yodels her way through "The Lonely Goatherd." That's okay. *Vive la différence!* You might be surprised by the fascinating things you learn or at least have some good laughs at some of your *Odd Couple* idiosyncrasies.

Who knows? You might just discover some new insights about the special woman God has placed in your life. But I suspect the most important thing you'll discover is that, despite your differing preferences, your favorite thing is your Christ-centered friendship.

A friend loves at all times.
PROVERBS 17:17

Chapter 30

GUESS WHO'S COMING TO DINNER?
Avoiding the World's Germs

I recently attended a dinner party at Sea World in Orlando. The evening began with hors d'oeuvres, and guests mingled amid faux palm trees and a three-man calypso band. Women wore bright floral sundresses, and the men wore Hawaiian shirts. Suntans gleamed, white teeth flashed, and smoothies flowed freely.

The pièce de résistance was the appearance of a few Sea World residents such as a feathery white cockatoo and a talking parrot, plumed in royal blue, sunshine yellow, and crayon red. But the dinner guest who stole the show turned out to be a petite penguin about two webbed-feet tall. When I spotted him across a crowded room, it was love at first sight; my heart leapt, and I couldn't stifle my giddy excitement. I shot over to the orange-billed bird.

"Wow!" I exclaimed to the handler. "A penguin!

Can I pet him?"

"You sure can," she said as she encouraged her tuxedoed companion to step into petting range.

So with my plate of food in one hand, I knelt to pet the penguin with the back of my other hand. Satisfied with touching Mr. P.'s soft feathery quills, I stood and deposited a mushroom au gratin in my kisser. At that moment, the bird made his own deposit on the tile floor. The handler nonchalantly wiped up the penguin puddle like a doting mommy with a burp rag.

"Sorry about that." She smiled apologetically. "He's really *full* of it tonight."

"So I see," I mumbled and excused myself, bypassing the smoothie bar, which suddenly lost its appeal.

That slump in appetite didn't last long, and I enthusiastically found a place at a white-clothed table. The woman next to me turned with a delighted smile on her face.

"Have you seen that darling penguin?" she asked.

"Yes, I have," I answered. "Pretty cute."

I'd lost some of my original enthusiasm after discovering the only guest who was wearing a tuxedo wasn't potty trained. "Did you pet him?" I casually inquired.

"Yes, I did!" She beamed, taking a bite of her salad. "I

thought he was adorable. Did you pet him?"

"I did!" I admitted, putting on an enthusiastic smile. "His feathers were softer than I had imagined. But did it occur to you that it wasn't exactly the epitome of hygiene to be petting an exotic bird while eating appetizers?"

"Oh dear, yes!" My dinner partner began to look a little worried, so I offered a tip for the next time she had dinner with a penguin. "Just pet him with the back of your left hand," I replied, pleased by my cleverness.

The lady was impressed. "Wish I'd thought of that!" she mumbled with a hint of angst.

I felt proud for having been a forward-thinking trendsetter in bird–hors d'oeuvres hygiene. Apparently the lady from my table was a talker, because for the rest of the mixer, I noticed partygoers backhanding the penguin with one hand while feeding themselves with the other.

One can't be too careful in these days of exotic viruses, but it's even more important to protect our souls in our morally contaminated culture. This requires some progressive thinking. We may need to research movies before mentally consuming images and words that replay in our minds long after the lights go up. Books, articles, videos, and Web sites can also condition us to accept values contrary to God's Word. It's not that we can't enjoy life's dinner party. We just need to be careful about what we pick up to eat and where.

Religion that God our Father accepts as pure and faultless is this:...to keep oneself from being polluted by the world.
JAMES 1:27

Chapter 31

BIRD OF PRAY
God in Unexpected Places

When I was a young single gal with a robust appetite and a lean dating life, I decided to take up running to prevent certain body parts from spreading. I wanted to enhance both my body and my odds for meeting Mr. Right. But the way things were going, I was well on my way to becoming the next Mrs. Jack Sprat. It was clearly time to spring into action.

I had just moved to Virginia, and my running routes wound through gorgeous tree-lined neighborhoods with pines that reached to the sky. The sun flickered through those tall branches, and I felt close to heaven whenever I gazed upward, letting the rays drench my face with their warmth.

On one particularly beautiful spring morning, hundreds of pink and white azalea bushes were in breathtaking bloom. I felt as if I were jogging through a dense, colorful wonderland of cotton candy.

I was so overtaken by the sheer glory of the moment, I began to sing: "Praise God from whom all blessings flow, praise Him all creatures. . ." I belted out every word, my heart soaring. Just as I was feeling rather Snow Whitey and about to exhort the woodland creatures to chime in, I felt a thump on my shoulder. I stopped to make sure I hadn't been shot with a BB gun by a naughty neighborhood hooligan.

Instead, I noticed approximately two tablespoons of white, green-flecked gunk oozing down my shoulder, staining my brand-new running shirt. This was *not* the thanks I expected from the Lord of Creation upon breaking into song for Him. Cautiously, I glanced skyward to see an egret gracefully (now that he had lightened his load) gliding through the sunlit sky. I began to laugh. "God," I prayed, "You sure have a weird sense of humor."

I don't know about you, but occasionally I feel God doesn't respond to me in quite the way I expect. During that fateful jog, I was innocently expressing my gratitude to Him for life and, ironically, for *nature*. And what did I get? Bird poop on my shoulder. And I was irritated with God for a nanosecond.

But I also got a reminder that God often uses

humor to show me He's a real Person with a full range of emotions—and I felt closer to Him for having made me laugh. And I also got the message that the Creator can rain down all kinds of things from heaven to get His children's attention and prompt their prayers and praise.

Every good and perfect gift is from above,
coming down from the Father.
JAMES 1:17

Chapter 32

FEELING CAMPY
The Joys of Interdependence

When my son, Trevor, was a tiger cub (not a real one—the Boy Scout kind), I volunteered to take him on his first camping trip. I enjoy the great outdoors and, as a youngster, secretly admired Euell Gibbons, the twig-eating naturalist and spokesman for Grape Nuts cereal. So this trip was right up my alley. However, when it comes to preparation, I'm more of a "wing it" woman than a "bring it" broad. I figured, *How much stuff could one mother and a six-year-old boy possibly need for a sleepover in the wild?*

As my son and I approached the campsite and saw other campers pitching tents and hanging Coleman lanterns, I began to feel outdoorsy. I gnawed on a twig and found it hard to believe that Euell had advocated this as snack food. The more I compared the vans crammed full of state-of-the-art outdoor gear with my compact car and duffle bag, the more insecure I felt about my packing job.

Thankfully, my friend Faith turned up and introduced me to her friend. "Rachel, this is Lynn Earle. Anything you need, she's got!" Lynn looked amazingly attractive in a khaki outfit that would make the normal woman resemble a zookeeper. Camper Barbie assessed my wadded-up tent and tiny cooler. "Need some help?" she offered.

Minutes later, my tent up and Ranger Lynn at my side, I felt more at ease. At dinnertime, I pulled out a raw hot dog and hunted for a stick to roast it on. When I returned, Lynn sat by the campfire roasting not one, not two, but *three* frankfurters skewered on a piece of ironwork that resembled King Neptune's trident.

"My husband made this," she said with a smile. I was happy for her, but I felt a twinge of "roasting envy," which kicked into high gear when my stick caught on fire. It would have taken more than dental records to identify the charred remains of my dinner as having once been a wiener.

As night fell, the early spring air turned progressively frigid. In our tent, we rolled around like human Popsicles wrapped in sleeping bags until 4:00 a.m., when I heard Faith's car motoring toward civilization and a warm bed. Trevor and I stuck it out, but I wanted to strangle every chirping, cooing, and trilling creature adding to the misery of the wee-hour arctic blast.

The payoff, however, was breakfast. I had packed Ding Dongs and milk but could smell pancakes cooking nearby. Cindy Camping Crawford looked at my Ding Dongs and tried to conceal her pity. "Care for some pancakes?" she asked. I felt like a grateful drifter as I hugged a cup o' java and savored every sweet bite of pancake around the warm campfire.

"Lynn," I called out, licking syrup from my fingers. "I appreciate you taking me under your wing, but I feel like a freeloader. How can I ever repay you?"

"Hey, don't even think about it!" she replied, laughing. Then she added with a gleam in her eye, "Come to think of it, there *is* something you can do for me. Toss me one of those Ding Dongs, will you?"

I could feel the first sparks of friendship igniting. This was my kind of gal—even if she looked better than I did in khaki (or anything else).

In our self-sufficient society, it seems taboo to express a need for anything or anyone. However, God often prefers interdependence over independence. With independence, you get you, yourself, and, well, you again. But interdependence gives us the opportunity to share the abundance that God has given us or to receive from someone else's abundance. And often we make a new friend along the way.

All the believers were one in heart and mind.
No one claimed that any of their possessions was
their own, but they shared everything they had.
Acts 4:32

Chapter 33

WHAT'S IN A NAME?
Reinventing Yourself Spiritually

My dad is a history buff. This sounds like an admirable trait in a man. But when I was young, Dad would hold our family hostage on summer vacations in our green station wagon (that we not-so-lovingly called the Pickle) while he hunted down every historical marker along the sun-drenched highway.

"Heeey, kids," Dad would croon with enthusiasm. "There's another historical marker in just ten miles!"

The prospect of enduring yet another historical carjack sent shivers up our short spines. My sister, brother, and I dreaded the thought of one more detour that would stretch our three-hour trip to about six. Based on our anguished protests, Mom called these bouts with history "hysterical markers."

On one memorable trip, we parked the Pickle at a roadside park in the picturesque town of Whitman,

Texas. While my siblings and I wistfully eyed the swings and slide, Dad morphed into General George E. Arnold and led his travel-weary troops headlong into the Battle of Boredom. As we fought to keep our hands to ourselves, Dad, invigorated by the smell of history in the air, propped his cowboy boot upon a large statue of an old guy with a beard and read with Gettysburgish zeal, "James T. Hogg served as county judge from 1896 to 1898. He and his wife, Mary, were residents of Whitman along with their daughter, Ima."

We sat in stunned amazement, not so much at the thought of a girl going through life with the name of Ima Hogg, but at our father, who opted for this pit stop over dip cones at Dairy Maid. In spite of my dip-cone dreams being dashed by roadside history, I thought, *Even if Ima were a babe, it must have been awful to have the name Hogg*.

Over the years, I've often thought of Ima Hogg and how hard it can be to drop the heavy saddlebags of a past persona. Some of us go through life feeling as if our names should have been Ima Loser, Ima Goner, or Ima Mess. But it doesn't have to be that way.

God has always been in the business of rewriting personal history, changing our names to reflect our new hearts. For example, remember wishy-washy Peter? He eventually became the Rock. So as God transforms your heart, why not claim a new name to reflect the new you? How about Ima Winner, Ima Gonnamakeit, or maybe Ima Not-So-Bad-After-All? With God's help, Ima sure you can do it!

You will be called by a new name that the mouth of the LORD will bestow. You will be a crown of splendor in the LORD's hand.

ISAIAH 62:2–3

THE ICE CREAM MAN COMETH
Fear, Faith, and a Changing World

I cherish the childhood memory of the sweet music ringing out from an ice cream truck. At the first faint note of "Three Blind Mice," my heart began to race, and I ran through the house frantically looking for Mom and a shiny dime. We lived on a court, and I can still remember the flood of relief I felt when I found the ice cream truck at a standstill, with the ice cream man filling orders for half a dozen neighbor kids. My treasure secured, I would sit with my buddies on the curb in front of my house, peeling the chocolate coating off our Eskimo Pies, letting it melt slowly on our tongues.

Well, those wonder years are far behind me now, and past Popsicles seem to have melted into a permanent part of my behind. Consequently, I do penance for pleasures past and present by jogging each afternoon in my neighborhood around 4:00 p.m. Recently

I heard the faint music of "The Entertainer" and was pleased to see that the ice cream truck still cometh. Upon first sighting the big white truck, I took a pleasant momentary trip down memory lane. But on subsequent outings, I've digressed into a suspicious frame of mind.

A lot of construction is going on in our neighborhood, and many vacant lots are sprinkled among the completed homes. For some reason, the ice cream man seems to crisscross my running route, and I start feeling eerily vulnerable as I hear the truck approaching the street I'm on. To make matters worse, from a distance, the driver looks like Popeye's nemesis, Brutus—a *big, burly* kind of guy.

In my moments of insecurity, I think, *Hmm. I wonder if that guy is really selling ice cream or if he's cruising for unsuspecting, slightly overweight women who can't run very fast.* Cleverly, I wave to an imaginary neighbor in the distance and holler, "Hi, Bob!" so it appears I'm being noticed and would be sorely missed if I suddenly disappeared.

Then I mentally rehearse a personal safety plan so that if—God forbid—the ice cream man tried to drag me into his truck, I would be ready. First, I would grab two fudge pops and shove them into his eyes. While he was flinging frozen globs of chocolate mush from his perverted peepers, I'd grab the microphone to the truck's sound system and yell, "Free ice cream! Hurry!" In a matter of seconds, mommies and kiddies would run out of nowhere like the Amish answering a clanging bell for help from a neighboring farm—and I would be rescued. After the cops dragged the ice cream criminal away, I would dole out free frozen treats from the back of the truck. I would receive a badge of courage from the mayor while the news cameras rolled and strains from the *Rocky* theme song blared over the truck's speakers.

And then, feeling a little sheepish, I wonder: *Maybe the ice cream man is a nice guy who is working a second job to make ends meet for his family. Maybe he's a big, burly man because, well, he likes ice cream. And maybe he crisscrosses my running route because it happens to be his* route.

And yet, times have, indeed, changed since I was a kid. We do have to focus more on personal safety. But does this relegate us to live a life of fear? Maybe our goal as believers should be to strike a balance between reasonable readiness and unflinching faith that God is our Protector.

So the next time you're tempted to dwell on a worst-case scenario, give it to God in prayer. Then look for the nearest place to chill out with your favorite ice cream cone.

"Do not let your hearts be troubled.
You believe in God; believe also in me."
JOHN 14:1

Chapter 35

OPPOSITES DISTRACT
Trying New Things

My sister and I have a *unique* relationship. Becky is a smidgen older than I am and more carefree. She's the kind of woman who says, "Let's try it and see what happens!" I'm the kind of woman who says, "What's the worst thing that could happen if we try this?"

Despite her laissez-faire flair, Becky can sell an idea whether it's good or not. She's so convincing that I'm certain she could sell a horsefly to a cow. So with a little trepidation, I mulled over Becky's invitation to spend a weekend with her at a bed-and-breakfast. My concerns stemmed from hearing stories of interesting experiences at B&Bs—things like eccentric hosts with unblinking eyes and rooms that lose half their square footage upon opening a suitcase. Apparently in the world of bed-and-breakfasts, quaint can be loosely defined.

Since I was knee-deep in ankle-biters and dirty dishes, the idea of a little distraction—escaping preschool purgatory for any reason—was quite appealing. So in spite of my reservations about staying in the home of complete strangers who never blink, I accepted my sister's offer.

The next day Becky read the brochure to me in her best Vanna voice: "Enter the Rose Garden Bed-and-Breakfast. Guests will enjoy a 1,000-square-foot suite, private porch with hot tub, and fluffy oversized bathrobes."

Immediately on guard, my mind began to drift. I visualized a splintered, weathered wooden porch surrounding a bubbling hot tub teeming with bacteria. Our innkeeper was the spitting image of Kathy Bates, and we were starring in our own version of *Misery*. I shook my head and came to just in time to hear Becky sign off: "This is going to be so much *fun!*"

Well, you know what? It *was* fun. Our suite was furnished with cushy couches and glowing flames in the fireplace. The stress of diapering and dish washing melted the moment I walked into the room. While I warmed a bit of apricot cider, Ms. Trusting Optimist plopped into the hot tub—floating around like a happy marshmallow in a vat of hot chocolate. I took a swig of my cider, threw caution to the wind, and dived in after her. My bacterial concerns were instantly quelled by the sighting of an albino leaf bubbling about and by the reassuring aroma of chlorine.

Giggling through the weekend with Pollyanna personified, I was fascinated by how different we were and yet how much we enjoyed being together. I realized that God often uses others' differences to push us out of our comfort zones. Once freed from our cozy cocoons, we become open to experiences that can bless us, mature us, and give us opportunities to meet others' needs.

So the next time a crazy friend asks you to try something new, why not give it a shot? You may just find yourself in hot water—relaxing in a hot tub on a weekend getaway.

The body is not made up of one part but of many. . . .
If they were all one part, where would the body be? . . .
Now you are the body of Christ, and each
one of you is a part of it.
1 CORINTHIANS 12:14, 19, 27

Chapter 36

BELLY UP
Accepting Things We Cannot Change

Many of my friends who have had babies within the last ten years are still preoccupied with their tummies. For most of us, the sad twist of nature is that, during pregnancy, your middle enlarges like a watermelon on growth hormones, and when the baby is born, your midriff stays inflated, as if you're carrying a permanent water balloon. Optimistic, sunshiny women endearingly pat their doughy development, dubbing it a "pooch," but realistic women call it like it is—a pot belly.

Although we like to talk about getting tummy tucks, most of us won't. Hey, if you have a discretionary five thousand dollars sitting around the house, you're sure to have at least one kid who needs braces or a husband who needs gutters. So we water-bellied wonders try to make peace with our inner balloon.

If you're still coming to terms with your expanded

midsection, I offer a recent experience that may be of help. One evening I filled my bathtub fairly high and made sure the water was toasty warm so I could get all the kinks out of the ol' bod (except for those wrinkles and stretch marks, which apparently are *permanent*). I sighed with contentment but soon fixated on my jelly belly.

How much extra fat and tissue is really here? I wondered. Then I scooched down in the tub, my head barely above water, and wadded my excess tummy in both hands. When I looked down again, I made an extraordinary discovery. As my belly button flattened into a straight line, I realized I was staring at the eyeless face of a Cabbage Patch Doll.

The beauty of this revelation is that although most of us who have given birth do not have tightly tucked tummies, we have fairly *fun* tummies—tummies with charisma. Think of it as having instant Play-Doh always on hand (or on belly). Whenever you're bored (and alone), you can whip out your abdominal dough and mold it into entertaining shapes.

You simply have to get into the same mind-set you'd need to see shapes in the clouds. Some of my favorites are the one-hump camel, the two-hump camel, the shar-pei puppy, and the manatee. I'm sure you can discover your own favorites and, in the process, make peace with your pooch—at least until you have a cool five thousand dollars on hand for a tummy tuck. But by then, you'll probably be tempted to buy stock in support hose and denture cream.

Many things in life can't be altered without a great deal of pain or money. That's a sobering thought for many of us who like snappy remedies for pesky problems. But we can do *something*. We can belly up to our problems, face them head-on, and ask God to help us find contentment in spite of them. He'll help us put unchangeable things in perspective. So the next time you face something that can't be changed easily, why not ask God to give you "new eyes" to find contentment in all circumstances?

God, grant me the serenity to accept the things
I cannot change, courage to change the things
I can, and wisdom to know the difference.
SERENITY PRAYER

Chapter 37

SOCKING AWAY LIFE'S GOODIES
Choosing a Colorful Life

For most mommies, part of the joy of having a little girl is shopping for outfits and accessories that transform their mini-me into a flamboyant fashion plate. For some women, this aspect of parenting a girl is a really big deal, and one peek into the wee one's closet reveals a wardrobe that would make Liberace swoon.

On that score, I must confess I am a bit of a tomboy. At my age, the more accurate terminology might be tommom. My first child was a boy, and I had so much fun dressing him in tiny Hawaiian shirts, plaid Bermuda shorts, and diminutive deck shoes that I wasn't sure I had what it took to dress up a little girl.

To my relief, I had eight years between Trevor and my daughter Tori to prepare for the task. This was just enough time for several trendy baby clothiers to emerge on the scene. By the time Tori arrived, I decided

I could dress a girl my way—not with bows and ruffles and dainty things but with cottony, sporty, *fun* clothes that seemed just right for someone set on rummaging through wastebaskets and toilets every time I turned my back.

It seemed my destiny to regularly shop the sales racks at Baby Gap and Gymboree. I became the Imelda Marcos of baby socks—not just any old socks, mind you, but those in stylish shades like cantaloupe, tangerine, banana, and kiwi. Tori had the fruitiest feet in our family. However, one day I opened her sock drawer and, to my horror, found a dozen fruit-named socks without a single mate!

Since I'd invested time and treasure in coordinated outfits for my precious pumpkin, I turned my house upside down, determined to find at least one matching sock. In a desperate moment, I opened the refrigerator and looked in the crisper in case they had mysteriously turned into *real* cantaloupes and tangerines. My search was fruitless.

Worse yet, I had to take my "happening" little girl out on the town with a banana on one foot and a kiwi on the other. I was so embarrassed that I put on a huge pair of Jackie Onassis sunglasses and prayed that passersby would think I was temporarily colorblind. Tori, however, seemed quietly unaffected as she removed her shoes and socks and sucked on her toes. Later that day, an unimaginative mother of a baby boy offered me this boring advice: "Buy all white socks."

Okay, so that counsel was practical. But do you really think God wants us to live a vanilla-bland life when He's made a thirty-one-flavors world? I doubt it. I think God wants us to color our world with rainbow colors and Willy Wonka flavors. Sure, playing it safe can make life easier (and duller), but branching out—even a little—can make life *fuller* (and more fun)!

"I have come that they may have life,
and have it to the full."
JOHN 10:10

Chapter 38

SNOW WHITE WRITER
When Dreams Collide with Reality

In the early days of pursuing my writing dream, I imagined a future filled with long lunches at open-air cafés where, beneath the shade of a canvas umbrella, I would write travel articles between bites of chicken friand and sips of mango tea. Later in the day, I might jog, take a long bath, and finally read a good book snuggled under my down comforter.

Boy, did I have to wake up before my dream could come true! I found out right away that the idyllic writer's life would require some risk taking and dues up front. So with the encouragement of my well-published sister, I wrote an article about a trip we took together. I hoped to capture an editor's attention by breaking the staid travel mold with offbeat observations woven throughout the piece. I figured if I didn't bore those editors, they might give me a shot at writing an article for their magazines. I sent out thirty copies of my piece and vowed not to take the inevitable rejections too seriously—this was a game of odds, albeit "prayed-over" odds.

I received an array of responses, ranging from form letters to the most accepting rejection letters a gal could hope for. Then I got a letter from an editor at *Better Homes and Gardens*. Her name was Nina, and although she didn't have a place for my article, she thought my writing was at least mildly amusing, and she gave me a little assignment.

So, having never grown a single plant other than a pinto bean in a Dixie cup when I was in kindergarten, I accepted the assignment to write a seven-hundred-word story about garden tours. For weeks I tiptoed through tulips, danced among daffodils, and walked in rings around rosies, taking copious notes and eavesdropping on old ladies in wide-brimmed sun hats, trying to learn how to pronounce the Latin names of foliage and flora.

I was riding high on the enticing fragrance of what seemed to be inevitable success until Nina called. In her nice but direct way, she let me know she hated my first draft. I thought she was going to fire me, but she kept me on the project. Regardless, my dream was still alive.

Then my husband lost his job. And we lost almost all of our money. Then after eight years of using birth control with textbook results, I became pregnant—and we had no health insurance. After years of leased cars, new homes, and private schools, we moved to Texas to live with my parents.

If my dream were to come true now, it wouldn't be under optimum circumstances. So I waved good-bye to the ideal of tapping away at my keyboard in a mountaintop villa while songbirds trilled in the background and said hello to prayer and perseverance.

Although I've yet to experience the writing life I dreamed about in early days, I enjoy inklings of it. For example, I finally earned enough to purchase a laptop and have spent many contented hours writing at a local French bakery complete with tulip-filled window boxes. Overall, I'm just grateful to be in the game.

Have you cherished a long-hidden desire to accomplish something? If your life were over tomorrow, would you regret not having tried? Are you still waiting for perfect timing and conditions? Why not take incremental steps? Spend time with positive people you can share your dream with, and find support to pursue it. You may not reach your ideal goal, but you may get to experience the joy of just being in the game.

*Then Jesus told his disciples a parable to show
them that they should always pray and not give up.*
LUKE 18:1

Chapter 39

HAVE WORM, WILL TRAVEL
Make Time for Diversions

I have a confession to make. I'm in love with someone who's not my husband. Worse yet, he's a real worm. Why would I fall for someone like that? For starters, he's really cute. He drives this cool-looking apple car with a sunroof. And he's a TV star. His name? Lowly. Lowly Worm, to be exact.

Actually, it's not only Lowly that I love; I am enamored with the whole *Richard Scarry's Busy Town, USA*. Something is exhilarating about watching this animated town come to life. Mice chefs crank out piping hot loaves of bread from a muffin-shaped boulangerie, and kitten children dressed in pinafores and suspenders walk paw in paw to the little red schoolhouse with a bell on top.

But Lowly really captures my imagination. This engaging earthmover is always going off on some adventure around the globe. Better yet, he has a matching hat and shoe for every locale. He sets sail for the Caribbean wearing a scuba mask and fin. For an expedition to Egypt, he wears a turban and a thong (the *sandal* kind). And when he climbs the Swiss Alps, he dons a feathered cap and a hiking boot. Not only is he cute; he's fashionable. He's like the Yves St. Laurent of worms. How can a woman resist a guy like that, I ask you?

On any given morning when facing yet another bowl of Cheerios and feeling not so cheery as I eye mounds of laundry, I can mentally drift off to the south of France with a debonair worm in a beret and penny loafer. It's a harmless diversion, really. Some women read romance novels; I live the exciting life of a world traveler through a crustacean without the crust. We all need a change of venue to temporarily escape the relentless responsibilities and hair-raising challenges of life. That's one reason why we look forward to going on vacation with such kineticism—we simply need a break from time to time.

In a spiritual sense, we need diversions, too. As we travel through our days, we never know when troubles—big or small—might erupt on the scene, threatening to sink our spirits and sabotage our faith.

God understands this dynamic. That's why He gave us scripture and the Holy Spirit—to refresh and redirect our travel-worn spirits.

So, fellow traveler, in Lowly style, grab a backpack, a Bible, and a pair of hiking boots, and determine to stay the course with your Travel Guide. No doubt He will lead you, with faith intact, to a destination that's out of this world!

"I have told you these things, so that in me you may have peace. In this world you will have trouble. But take heart! I have overcome the world."
JOHN 16:33

Chapter 40

YOU DIRTY RAT!
Money, Marketing, and You

"Hey!" Tiff announced enthusiastically. "Did you know you can get a souvenir cup with the purchase of a soft drink at Mr. Cheesy's Pizza Parlor—for a limited time only—for the low, low price of a greenback? *And* [I could almost hear the drum roll] you get free refills!"

It seemed like a good idea at the time, so Tiff and I loaded kids in our vans and headed for Mr. Cheesy's, where cheap, thrill-seeking patrons like us could sip soft drinks from a souvenir cup shaped like Mr. Cheesy Mouse himself. Cute mouse, free refills—what's not to love?

While watching the stage show of robotic gyrating rats, mice, and break-dancing chickens, I ate pizza and sipped from my nifty plastic-molded mouse cup. As I withdrew the straw from my lips, a strange realization hit me: The straw was actually Mr. Cheesy's tail. I blinked and looked at Tiff.

"How gross is this?" I demanded. "I'm sipping cola through the tip of a rat's tail!" After I studied my drink, thirst overcame me. "Ah, well," I sighed. "Bottoms up."

My astute cohort remarked passionlessly, "Yeah, now that you mention it, it's very unattractive." She glanced around the showroom to make sure her rug rats were still scurrying nearby, then offered, "I'm going for a refill. Want anything? Cola? Juice? Rat poison?"

"Yeah," I countered, "can you bring me a friend who won't suggest kiddy outings that cause me to do unseemly things in public?"

We giggled but have since then talked about the constant pressure in our culture to spend money on dumb things. It's so easy to let our values become topsy-turvy. Notice how the lure of marketing often makes something look like fun at first glance, but it may not be in the best taste—or even in good judgment. Then the next thing we know, we go places or do things we never intended—like sipping soda through a rat's tail—and realize we've bottomed out, pardon the pun.

In a fast-paced world driven by marketing mavens who make their living at our expense, we may need to analyze the whole picture before stepping into their lure, or mousetrap, as the case may be.

Thankfully, God has given us His Holy Spirit, His Word, and trusted friends to help us discern the good from the not-so-good. These things can help us navigate the maze of TV commercials and billboards without falling into the marketers' clever traps and finding our budgets nibbled to a nubbin. The more we make better choices, the less we'll say, "Rats! I wish I hadn't done that!"

Houses and wealth are inherited from parents,
but a prudent wife is from the LORD.
PROVERBS 19:14

Chapter 41

A SHARP COOKIE
Defining the Shape of Your Life

My eleven-year-old son, Trevor, and I were returning from a jaunt to the grocery. As is our custom, we rifled through the bags of food to sustain us for the journey ahead—a ten-minute drive through suburbia. "Gee, Mom, didn't you buy any good stuff?" Trevor asked.

Hope almost gone, he suddenly spied a box of animal cookies lying at his feet. *What luck!* I thought. And he, like a hunter presenting his catch upside down by its ankles, asked brightly, "Want some?"

"Sure!" I shot back. "Let's see what you bagged, kid."

It may seem juvenile, but animal cookies have been a favorite of mine since childhood. I especially like the kind in a small rectangular box depicting teeth-baring lions, tigers, and bears in a red-and-gold circus wagon. As a youngster, I immediately scarfed down the cookies in one sitting, then, feeding frenzy behind me, could appreciate the box's nifty string handle. It had a nice, sturdy feel to it. While other little girls used the box for a purse to house their makeup, I used it to shelter my bug collection. But onward with the Cookie Safari at hand. . .

"Here's an elephant," Trevor announced as he handed me the cookie.

"That looks more like a camel to me," I remarked. "On second thought, it doesn't look like an animal at all."

"Well, what did you expect? You bought the cheapo brand!"

"Yeah, yeah, champagne taste," I muttered under my breath. Then I said, "Well, as strange as it sounds, I guess I expected animal cookies to look like, well. . . animals. Toss me that cheap box," I demanded while decapitating the camelphant with my front teeth. "Look at these pictures. Now where are these animals?"

I pointed to a hippo twirling about in a tutu and a giraffe modeling a floor-length necktie. I shoved my hand into the box, pulled out a handful of cookies, and shoved them under my son's nose. Our chitchat quickly degenerating into drivel, we ended up with a bad case of the giggles.

Trevor looked more closely at the rounded, face-less shapes in my palm. "You're right, Mom," he chuckled.

"They don't look like *anything*." We agreed we had been bamboozled by this budget box of cookies that looked more like puffy albino clover than circus beasts.

So I learned my lesson and since then have splurged for the real McCoy. It's a small price to pay for the pleasure of systematically nipping off the heads and appendages of *real* animal cookies.

Don't get me wrong. Sometimes choosing the generic brand can be a great way to save denari. But when it comes to decisions *outside* the grocery store, we can get in a rut of making so many conservative choices that we never experience the soul-stirring joy of living out the desires of our hearts. As a result, our lives, like those cookies, resemble nondescript dry blobs rather than the well-sculpted, intentional shapes that God has in mind for us.

We have not stopped praying for you. We continually ask
God to fill you with the knowledge of his will.
COLOSSIANS 1:9

HOT DAY AT THE ZOO
When Life Gets Too Hot to Handle

My friend Judy made a serious mistake. She had moved from California to Texas during one of the hottest summers in recent memory, when the mercury soared to over one hundred degrees for a whole week. Translation for non-Texans: You can shellac your locks with an entire can of hairspray, pat on fresh makeup, and walk out your front door looking like Cameron Diaz, only to return minutes later having generated enough perspiration to resemble Tammy Faye Baker after a good cry in a soaking rain. So under these hothouse weather conditions, Judy's husband, John, suggested they take Max, their three-year-old, animal-lover son, to the zoo.

Now, granted, the zoo has lots of trees that provide a shady respite from the sun. But when temperatures soar that high, it doesn't matter if you're sitting on a block of ice—it's still hot. So the last time I met Judy for breakfast, I was curious to hear if they actually went through with their zoo plans.

"It was awful!" Judy wailed, rolling her eyes. "It was so hot, the animals wouldn't even come out."

"So did you cut your losses and leave?" I asked between bites of my cheesy eggs and buttery grits.

"I wish!" she growled. "You know Max is addicted to that Safari Dude television show and was determined to see a real, live jungle animal. So we felt we had to stick it out, at least for a little while. We slugged through each animal-less exhibit until our feet felt like smoldering lead and our heads felt like wilting lettuce. I knew something had to give.

"So I pulled him aside and said, 'Sweetie, listen, it's burning up. We'll stay just long enough to find one jungle animal, okay?' Mercifully, before long, I spotted a stray yellow cat with grease spots on his coat next to a dumpster, pawing his way through a discarded bag of Cheetos. At that moment, I had a stroke of sheer genius.

" 'Look, Max! It's the Cheetos Cheetah! See him?'

"Max looked up at me, a twinge of doubt in his face. 'Are you sure, Mommy? He doesn't have any sunglasses, and he looks kind of small.'

" 'Sure it's him, sweetie,' I fibbed. 'He only needs his glasses when he's on TV, and television makes everyone look ten pounds heavier.' "

"Well, did he buy it?" I asked.

"Hook, line, and sinker!" Judy replied, beaming. "It made his day, and that made ours—we were soon on our way home, basking in the arctic blast of the A/C in our minivan!"

Later, I thought about my friend's hot day at the zoo. I realized we all experience times when, like those animals, life gets too hot to handle and we run for cover. The daily grind alone (bills to pay, bosses to please, pounds to lose) can generate enough heat to send many of us packing for our emotional caves. In the process, we may isolate ourselves physically or emotionally, and the resulting loneliness can be too much to bear (pardon the pun).

During those times, if we truly want to find inner joy again, we'll eventually have to venture out from our hiding places. If those animals had come out of their caves on that hot summer day, they'd have found a three-year-old admirer, eager to brighten their day. And on a human level, if we dare to be open about our too-hot-to-handle struggles, we will often find the same thing—a trustworthy friend who admires our honesty and will share the right words of encouragement to help us cool down and carry on.

Carry each other's burdens, and in this way you will fulfill the law of Christ.
GALATIANS 6:2

Chapter 43

JOCKEYING FOR POSITION
Our Plans vs. God's Plans

I once heard a preacher tell a story about an old sway-back mule in the Kentucky Derby. His belly almost touched the ground, and his jockey's feet weren't much higher. A fellow jockey, sitting astride a muscle-bound thoroughbred, towered above the diminutive duo. "You know he doesn't have a chance, don't you?" he called out.

"Oh, I don't expect him to win," the low rider responded. "I just thought the exposure would be good for him."

Many of us began adulthood with the confidence of a jockey astride a thoroughbred, ready to bolt through the starting gate of life and leave the competition in the dust. Yes, we were going to be one of the successful, beautiful people who rule the world, perhaps through medicine, law, politics, or the arts. We were going to live in the best neighborhoods, drive our kids to school in a Mercedes Benz, and attend parties with all the other beautiful people. Ah, the American dream. . .

Instead, most of us are sitting lower in the achievement saddle than we expected. Maybe Mr. Perfect came along before we finished college, and the next thing we knew, Perfect Jr. popped into the picture at a less-than-perfect time. Or maybe job loss or illness or something else interrupted our plans somewhere along the way. As a result, perhaps our feet drag the floor as we try to keep our dreams from buckling under us.

But maybe we can learn something from that jockey. It would have been easy for him to feel intimidated by the other jockey's superior attitude. He could have fallen headlong into that old familiar trap of comparing ourselves to others. He could have shaken in his riding boots, afraid of being the laughingstock of the derby. Let's face it: The guy wasn't exactly riding Seabiscuit; it was more like Sea Level. But he didn't let that get him down. Maybe he was in it for what he might learn along the racetrack of his journey instead of reaching the destination in record time.

The goals of life we had at the starting gate are rarely what God has in mind for us. Most of us will lead what appears to be an ordinary life. But if we're accomplishing our God-given mission in life, we are successful. And usually, we find we're content and often joyful.

As Henry Blackaby notes in the *Experiencing God* study, God is always at work in the world. Our part is to ask in prayer to be included.

God's call may vary in our lives from time to time. The call may be for a season until we go on to another. I have a mentor who's in her late sixties, and she and her husband retired to a spacious and comfortable home. There they've discovered that they haven't retired but that God has called them to a new thing. Weary folks seem to find unusual rest and refreshment and even healing in their inviting home. She says it's the happiest time of her life.

So the next time you feel you're riding the saggy-bellied mule of dashed dreams, shift your focus from the destination to the journey. Perhaps God has lessons, gifts, and ministry along the way that will put you on the track to a victorious finish line, no matter how the final bottom line may read.

For we are God's handiwork, created in Christ Jesus to do good works, which God prepared in advance for us to do.
EPHESIANS 2:10

Chapter 44

CLUMP-CLUMP CART

When Gunk Is Stuck on Your Life

One hectic morning, I dashed to the grocery store without makeup or other vital beauty enhancements. Feeling a bit self-conscious, I consoled myself with the idea that it should be easy to shop inconspicuously for such a short errand. And then I heard it. "Oh no, not again!" I whined aloud. The familiar *clump, clump, clump* confirmed my deepest fears. Yep, I had grabbed another clump-clump cart.

Most seasoned shoppers have at one time or another encountered a clump-clump cart. The cart limps along like a peg-legged pirate thanks to a clump of blackish gunk stuck to a wheel. This usually consists of an assortment of chewed gum in faded rainbow colors and mixed with human hairs so diverse an Olympic Committee would be proud.

So much for shopping unnoticed. I sounded like

an escapee from a chain gang. "Don't mind me—Cool Hand Luke here—just shoppin' for some aiggs," I quipped, hoping a little prison humor would melt my irritation.

As I clanged along, I decided that grocers share a tacit conspiracy. I was convinced that they actually order these carts with clumps attached. This way they save thousands of dollars on janitorial costs by having unsuspecting shoppers clean the floors with these "lint brushes" on wheels.

Looking around for someone to commiserate with, I spotted the immaculately kempt Ms. Crocker, smiling from her perch on the dry goods shelf. "You know, Betty," I said, "there's gotta be a lesson in this. I am so agitated by this lopsided cart that I feel like scraping that clump off with my bare hands and hurling it into the bakery."

Betty seemed unmoved by my emotional confession. For a moment, I envied her placid demeanor, but then a thought hit me like a clump out of the blue.

On a spiritual level (trust me, clump-clump carts are wrought with theological significance), I realized the unsightly, irritating clumps were metaphors for the troubles that attach themselves to the shopping cart of my life. When I try to remove the clumps myself, I end up with a black, hairy mess on my hands.

In the grocery store of life, I need to learn to call for the Manager when I face sticky issues. I should cry out to God, "Woman needs clump removal—aisle ten!" Then He would either reach down with His celestial X-Acto knife and remove the clump altogether or distract me with the pleasure of His company while I cruise life's shopping aisles with Him by my side.

"In your distress you called and I rescued you."
PSALM 81:7

Chapter 45

THE MONEY PIT
Let It Die, Already!

When money was tight, we considered buying an older car with only sixty thousand miles and a body that looked like new. Jacques, our mechanic from France, cautioned us: "Jou mus drive a car enough to keep zee rubber hoses and zee belts from cracking, Meeses St. John-Gilbair," he patiently explained. "Eef zee oil and lubrication 'ave not been changed regularly, zee engine, she may expire!" Jacques looked so foreboding, I almost lost my nerve.

But we needed a thriftier car. We reasoned that with all the money we would save on a new car payment, we would still be ahead, even if we made a few repairs. All we knew was we could afford it. So we sprang for it.

Before long, our mechanic turned prophet had his head permanently housed underneath the hood of our clunker. The hoses sprang leaks like they'd had a run-in with Al Capone over a spaghetti dinner in Little Italy. At one point the driver's sideview mirror simply dropped off. Ditto with the rearview mirror. Soon we couldn't open the driver's door without first opening the back door. And the beat went on. But all of this paled compared to the catastrophic loss of the essential equipment that a person must have to survive the Amazon humidity of Virginia summers: air-conditioning.

Although the A/C was a goner, I was in denial. I turned obsessively optimistic as I flipped the switch to HIGH every time I started the car. I guess I thought it might spontaneously leap to life one day. So with my hope alive and my A/C dead, I urged my husband to let the mechanic search for the definitive answer to our sauna-mobile nightmares. A few months and twelve hundred dollars later, I was sitting yet again in the waiting area of Jacques's garage.

The agony of waiting for the A/C prognosis was more excruciating than waiting for my husband to come out of hernia surgery. Jacques emerged from under the hood of the car and stepped into the waiting area, gently settling beside me.

"We be friends long time, no?" he gingerly began.

"Yes, too long," I joked, trying to soften the blow I knew was coming. He did not smile.

"Dis car," he said, sadly shaking his head, "dis car no good. I no can fix the air."

I slumped and accepted the inevitable. Yes, the car had turned out to be a great deal—a great deal of trouble and expense. We eventually gave it to a minister friend and his wife. A few months later, our friends called to tell us the car had died, to which I said (no, screamed), "Good riddance!"

Most of us, at one time or another, have possessions that turn into money pits. We shovel the dough in, hoping one more repair will do the trick. Too often we find ourselves singing "Nearer, My God, to Thee" while sinking on the ship of runaway costs.

Other things in life can be like that old clunker that we need to stop trying to revive and let die. The time may come with a project, a possession, or even a relationship when we just need to let go. Perhaps God will resurrect it later or give us something better, but if we don't want to find ourselves in the poorhouse or the nuthouse, we might be better off to leave the decision to Him.

There is a time for everything,
and a season for every activity under the heavens.
Ecclesiastes 3:1

Chapter 46

ALL COUPED UP
Recharging Your Batteries

I'm not sure a woman truly appreciates her minivan unless she's driven halfway across the country in the heat of summer in a two-door coupe—with three kids and a sick cat foaming at the mouth. So when our young family (the kids were young, anyway) traded coupe purgatory for van heaven, I was a happy driver, indeed.

My little piece of heaven on wheels is a cornflower blue Toyota Sienna. We got the souped-down model so we could still afford some Happy Meals in the future and passed on leather seats since body fluid control was still a problem for the youngest members of our road crew. Actually, fluid control of any kind was a concern. Someone needs to invent a lid that can't be opened by precocious toddlers who are bent on exploring ways to unleash the contents of their kiddie cups.

We've had our van for two years, and I still breathe

a sigh of relief every time I lower my padded derriere into the padded captain's chair. Just having a few feet instead of a few inches between me and my squirming, squealing crew diminishes my stress factor. How cool is it to pull over, walk the length of your vehicle with the A/C full blast, and tend to runny noses, sticky hands, and sibling uprisings (or occasional seat-risings) without opening the door? Take it from this former couped-up chauffeur: It's cooler than an ice sculpture of James Dean.

My kids and I have had countless tailgate meals in the rear of our van, colored enough pictures to open a Louvre for Little Ones, and spilled enough soft drinks to fill an Olympic-sized swimming pool. Yup, Old Blue is my baby—my lifeline to traveling sanity with loud (and sometimes leaping) Lilliputians.

It's amazing what a little space and good A/C can do for a harried mom on the road. Likewise, on the road of life, the day-to-day tasks and demands of family relationships can leave us feeling cooped up. Don't minimize the need to give your soul a little roaming room. You might even consider making arrangements to drive your mini to a local hotel and max out on books, music, and DVDs that set your spirit soaring. Or ask a friend to fly the coop with you for a pit-stop lunch and some insightful conversation. You may be surprised at how your tank will fill up, and in no time, you'll be ready to hit the road again.

So they set out from the mountain of the LORD and traveled for three days. The ark of the covenant of the LORD went before them during those three days to find them a place to rest.
NUMBERS 10:33

Chapter 47

CONVERTIBLE CONVERT
It's Good to Dream

"Hi! Welcome to the show. What's yah question?"

I was listening to National Public Radio's *Car Talk* while tooling down the road. I love listening to these sharp-witted, fifty-something brothers with New England accents. They dole out advice on all things auto, tucking in some good advice about life along the way. On this day, they were doing some good-natured bantering with a lady who sounded sweet and very conscientious.

"I have a Honda Accord that's five years old with only 28,000 miles on it," she began. "It's been such a reliable car, and I only drive it around town for errands. But lately I've been fighting the urge to buy a VW Beetle convertible. From what I've read, though, I understand there's no strong reliability record established yet."

"Furst of all, how old are yah?" the host asked then

quickly backed off. "Oops! Let's try this: Are you undah or ovah fifty?"

"Over fifty," she admitted.

"Buy the cah tomorrow!" he shot back. "There's not much *time*!"

They laughed heartily, and I chuckled right along with them.

"Okay," the lady replied, "I do have white hair, but it's not purple—yet." Obviously they were dealing with a young-at-heart, doggone good sport!

"Look," said Brother Number One, getting down to her question. "You don't really want advice; you just want to be able to tell your friends, 'Hey, those *Cah Tawlk* guys told me I should buy it.' Right?"

"It's not so much that," she hedged. You could feel her mounting angst. "I have this nagging thought in my mind that if I buy the Beetle, I'll regret it later."

At that point, Brother Number Two chimed in, "Yah not gonna regret it, honey! Listen, you can have pizzazz or reliability, but yah can't have 'em both. When my sistah-in-law married her husband, she thought she was gettin' reliability, but as it turns out, she only got pizzazz!"

We all had a good laugh on that one, and Number Two continued, "Seriously, fah-ged-a-bowd-it! Live a little! Buy the cah. Every time you get in it and put the top down, yah gonna smile."

"Okay!" She all but giggled. "And thank you!"

I could almost "see" her smile rakishly, ready to ride out her sunset years with convertible top down and wind blowing in her hair—the happiest fifty-plus woman in town.

Coincidentally, I had an e-mail from my mother awhile back, saying she has a new friend in her fifties. This artsy, stylish lady has just bought a snappy-looking silver convertible VW Beetle with a black canvas top. She invited Mom to go to breakfast one morning and said she'd pick Mom up. She did and had managed to place a yellow sunflower in the bud vase on her dashboard. She popped out of the car, ran to the passenger side, and swung the door open with a flourish for Mom to enter. Dad was clicking the camera from the front porch and exclaimed, "Now, *that's* my girl—young at heart and traveling in style!"

Whether or not we can financially support our desires and dreams, it's paramount that we acknowledge them and speak of them—to good friends, to our spouse, and, most importantly, to God. Often we find joy in simply speaking aloud those things that make our hearts flutter. If we can learn to hold our desires loosely and let God sift them through His all-knowing, all-loving hands, we will probably find some dreams coming true and others changing into something a little different. So dare to dream, and let God in on the brainstorming sessions!

*"I have come that they may
have life, and have it to the full."*
JOHN 10:10

Chapter 48

WORLD PIECE
Ruts and a Change of Venue

I'm writing this from the comforting haven of the Corner Bakery and Café, nursing a bad case of writer's block. Here, the ceilings soar overhead and milk chocolate tones of stained oak outline beveled glass windows. The floors are checkerboard black-and-white tile; the pastry case brims with icing-drizzled apple streusel, lemon bars, mini carrot cakes, and just about anything else you could want to soothe your sweet tooth or restless soul. The syncopated happy notes of swing music play quietly in the background. Add to that a hearty cup of fresh-roasted whole bean coffee, and you have the next best thing to heaven.

I've done well until this last week before the deadline. When I gleefully signed the contract to this quirky first volume o' mine, I was going to show all those other publishers who had turned me down a thing or two. Yep, I was going to write like the Queen of Quirk, Anne Lamott, and mine the depths of spiritual truth like the Princess of Peace, Beth Moore. The problem is that my offbeat is off, my quirky won't quirk, and my faith is shaky as I wonder how in heaven's name I'm gonna finish this book.

I called a seasoned writing pal to commiserate. It helped a little. She said, "Rachel, it's like the last weeks of pregnancy when we're ambling around like Quasimodo and are pretty sure the condition is permanent. We feel we'll never get that baby born, but somehow we do." She then added, "Get out of the house and go somewhere that gets your creative juices flowing." So here I am, feeling surprisingly mellow and ready to dive back in.

As I sit here getting my groove back, I think maybe I've discovered the secret to successful foreign relations. Perhaps the international symbol for world peace should be a cup of coffee and a pastry. It would seem difficult, if not impossible, for the world's leaders to be cranky with each other when enjoying fresh-roasted coffee and flaky apricot streusel.

Take, for example, the UN. How can we expect to foster goodwill among irritable ambassadors when the only thing served at the sessions is a boring glass of water? Just the thought of listening to endless speeches in hundreds of foreign languages while sipping mere H_2O makes me grumpy.

On the other hand, imagine this: Mr. Kofi Annan strides to the podium to open a meeting.

"Welcome to the UN," he says in that charming accent. "Our coffee of the day is a full-bodied Sumatra roast paired beautifully with lemon chiffon tarts. And for your listening pleasure, please tune your headsets to radio station KLUV and enjoy the playful sounds of American swing. Alrighty then. Praise the Lord and pass the resolutions!" It would certainly work—if all the delegates were women.

But back to ordinary you and me. Maybe you're stuck in a rut and feel there's no way out. Perhaps you don't have writer's block, but maybe you've reached the saturation point with a project at work, or toilet training a toddler (or a live-in elderly relative!), or going toe-to-toe with a teenager with attitude. Sometimes we just need a change of venue and time to reconnect with who we are and who God is so we can put things in perspective and carry on. If a visit to a bakery isn't your thing, find something that is. Maybe it's having a picnic at a botanical garden, or taking an upbeat friend to lunch, or getting some overdue exercise. Do whatever it takes to keep some peace and relaxation in your own little corner of the world.

There remains, then, a Sabbath-rest for the people of God;
for anyone who enters God's rest also rests from
their works, just as God did from his.
HEBREWS 4:9–10

Chapter 49

WHEN IT FEELS LIKE THE END IS NEAR
Sometimes It's Laugh or Cry

Our family has had one of "those weeks." The pediatrician has renamed Waiting Room #3 "the St. John-Gilbert Suite." For starters, Trevor came home from football practice with a baseball-sized lump on his ankle. Then Tori developed a sty that forced her eyelid half shut. And I developed a bump on the roof of my mouth that Super Endodontist Man says is a slow but sure abscess—*cha-ching!*

Not to be left out, baby Whitney decided to join the parade of injured persons. The other morning, I left Trevor upstairs to elevate his sprained ankle while Tori watched cartoons with eyelid at half mast. Whitney was in her playpen, contentedly tickling the plastic ivories of her baby grand. Meanwhile, I had just hunkered down into a hot bath, savoring what I hoped to be at least fifteen glorious minutes alone.

"Mooom!" Trevor's voice carried with amazing clarity down the steps and through the crack under my bathroom door. I grabbed my robe and ran upstairs to find Whitney crying, mouth open wide and dripping blood at a concerning, yet thankfully slow, pace.

"I'm sorry!" Trev's lip trembled. "She was getting fussy, so I let her out and she hit her mouth on the coffee table."

Amazingly, Whit didn't seem to be in that much pain, although Trevor testified to an excruciatingly long silent scream followed by the real thing, of course. Throughout the rest of the day, every time she flashed her precious smile (my mother calls it a benediction), she looked like Count Dracula Baby after a fruitful night on the town.

Toward evening, I took stock. *Hmm. . .let's see now,* I calculated. *We now have a gimpy son, a three-year-old whose face is a troubling hybrid of Audrey Hepburn and the Hunchback of Notre Dame, and a baby who has permanently severed that funky piece of skin that connects her upper lip to her gum.* All in a day's work—for the guy in the black hood, that is. For a moment, I wished I had the gumption of some of my charismatic friends to shout aloud, "Go to h-e-double-hockey-sticks, you devil!" And in my own way, I did. I have put "the punk of darkness" on notice that my kids belong to the Light of the World. And I have spent more time praying to that effect.

And then I received news that made my week pale in comparison to my good friend's. Bonnie's nineteen-year-old nephew, a star baseball player at his college, answered his door Thursday night and was blown away—literally—into the next life. No known motive, no suspect, no undoing what is done.

Ironically, Bonnie has been one of those optimistic "producers" in my life who always uses her difficulties for good. *So how will she handle this?* I wondered. The answer came quickly. Although the enemy has his heavy foot on her throat right now, he doesn't know that a bad guy can't keep a good woman down for long. She will grieve. But I know she will wrestle free from the temptation to fall headlong into her dark pit of sorrow—and stay there. She will eventually find healing, hope, and victory in Jesus. In time, she will even have days when she will wake up laughing—to the glory of God, to the honor of her nephew's memory, and to the inspiration of believers like you and me.

If you're facing heartache, follow a path to healing—wherever it may lead you. Don't despair. When the time is right, God will restore your ability to laugh with others and with Him. Conversely, if your heart is full from the blessings God has rained on you lately, revel in this season of joy, and let your laughter reverberate to the heavens.

A cheerful heart is good medicine,
but a crushed spirit dries up the bones.
PROVERBS 17:22

That the Christian weeps we need no theory or argument or
evidence. The cross is sufficient to command our tears. Praise
be to God that it also is sufficient to command our laughter.
TERRY LINDVALL

Sources

Coulter, Lynn. "Fingerprint." *Sky* magazine. Greensboro, N.C., July 2003.

Eisenberg, Lawrence. "Caine Scrutiny." *AARP* magazine. Washington, D.C., May/June 2003.

Eldridge, John. *Wild at Heart.* Nashville: Thomas Nelson, 2001.

Lindvall, Terrence. *The Mother of All Laughter: Sarah and the Genesis of Comedy.* Nashville: Broadman & Holman, 2003.

About the Author

Rachel's family includes husband, Scott, and three kids who love to perform. Trevor is a music theater major at The University of Michigan. Little sisters Tori and Whitney perform nightly to a sold-out crowd of two. Rachel's e-mail is writesjg@earthlink.net.